SCHOOL BOARDS

STRENGTHENING

GRASS · ROOTS

LEADERSHIP

The Institute for
Educational Leadership

Acknowledgements

This project benefited from the contributions of many individuals. It is impossible to list all of them but we do want to recognize those without whose involvement there could not have been a study or this report.

We are particularly grateful to Peter Goldberg, vice president of the American Can Company Foundation, for his substantive as well as financial assistance. Anne Lewis deserves a special thank you for her patience in editing the work of six authors. We want to thank Thomas Shannon, executive director of the National School Boards Association (NSBA), and Nellie Weil, president of NSBA, for their thoughtful Foreword, and Neal Peirce, contributing editor to *The National Journal* for his thought-provoking Preface.

We wish to thank also the several hundred board of education chairpersons and members who responded to the study questionnaire and the school boards which so readily agreed to be sites for the field-based case studies. We are grateful to Michael Thomas, Kristen Kask, Sister Anne Diederick and Emily Harbold at the Ohio State University who assisted in interviews and research during the study, to John Forrer who helped us with data analysis, and to Stina Santiestevan who provided a final, dispassionate edit.

Finally, we want to thank John Rankin who produced the many drafts, Robert Danzberger and Mary-Duke Smith who entered and brought forth all the questionnaire data, Louise Clarke who managed the production of all the drafts and shepherded the report to publication, and others on the IEL staff who supported our efforts.

Lila N. Carol

Jacqueline P. Danzberger

Barbara A. McCloud

Luvern L. Cunningham

Michael W. Kirst

Michael D. Usdan

Table of Contents

About This Report

Public elementary and secondary education is a priority issue for the nation's public policy debates. Education reform (or as we prefer, improvement) has stimulated extensive discussion about our schools—their structure and their quality, as delivered through a very decentralized education system.

So far, improvement has been stimulated by state policymakers. Governors and legislators, often buttressed by or responding to civic and business leaders, have initiated unprecedented efforts to improve the quality of public education.

For the most part, these state-level initiatives have bypassed local school boards. School boards feel they have, at best, been only peripherally involved, that they have been cast in a passive role and are perceived as reactors rather than partners in shaping changes.

Yet, the national agenda is now being recast as states try implementing recent policy initiatives and face the complexities of restructuring education at the school district and classroom levels. The success or failure of these efforts rests squarely with local school boards, teachers, administrators and communities. Because school boards are charged by states and localities to make policy and govern local public education, their willingness and capacity to lead, in large measure, will determine the long-range success or failure of school improvement efforts.

The nation moves into this second wave of education improvement efforts with some resentment at the local level. School boards along with classroom teachers and administrators feel they have not been consulted adequately or involved in the state education initiatives in the past few years.

Some critics of local educational leadership contend states were forced to take the initiative because school boards and local educators had abdicated their leadership responsibilities and were resisting change. Whether this criticism is valid or not is less important than the need for both local and state leaders to recognize we cannot afford to have winners and losers in a political tug-of-war over education. Society's stake in improving schools calls for the nation to be the winner and for there to be no losers.

The Institute for Educational Leadership (IEL) recognizes that the role of the local school board is pivotal to the success of school improvement efforts. Constructive changes will be implemented only if they are acceptable to locally perceived values and education needs. School boards, despite their local responsibility for governance, have received little systematic analysis or attention in recent years, and rarely has their crucial role been stressed in recent actions, discussions and debates at the state level, or in the many national reports on improving education. With the intent of redressing this omission, IEL received support from the American Can Company Foundation in the spring of 1985 to conduct a national study of the local school board. This report is the product of that study.

Readers will find in the report an executive summary and a summary of the findings (Chapter 2). Chapter 1 presents an overview of the study and results of the questionnaire. Chapter 3 discusses the role of school boards in American society, including a brief history of their evolution. In Chapter 4, on the working board, we discuss the challenges boards face in developing their operating structures. Chapter 5 explores the board-superintendent relationship, which influences community perceptions of the effectiveness of local leadership. The report probes, in Chapter 6, existing and emerging issues school boards face, including those affecting state-local relationships. We also explore both board members' and citizens' satisfactions and dissatisfactions with board practices and leadership roles (Chapter 7). The need for increased attention to school board development for individuals, even more importantly, for the board as a whole is stressed in Chapter 8, along with recommendations to remedy existing weaknesses.

In the final chapter, we present fifteen indicators of an effective board. This framework is offered as a starting point for boards and their communities to assess current policies and practices and to strengthen board leadership.

We found strong support among community leaders, parents, local citizens and educators for the institution of local school boards. As we moved out from this city by the Potomac, we found citizens do **not** believe school boards are "dinosaurs left over from our agrarian past," as has been suggested by some national observers. We did, however, find consensus, even among many school board leaders, that school boards need to be strengthened and must carefully look at their weaknesses if they are to exercise effective, positive leadership during this unique time of opportunity for improving American education.

Michael D. Usdan
President
Institute for Educational
  Leadership

Jacqueline P. Danzberger
Director, Local Improvement Programs
Project Director
Study of Local Boards of Education

Washington, D.C.
October, 1986

This report from the Institute for Educational Leadership (IEL) is significant for three reasons:

☐ In a period of close inspection of elementary and secondary education across our nation and sometimes strident rhetoric calling for
the "restructuring" of the public schools, the local school board
emerges from the IEL study as the clearly preferred agency to
govern the schools in local communities. The overriding conclu-
sion of the IEL report is that the uniquely American institution of
representative and participatory government—epitomized by the
local school board—is the best vehicle for the people to keep
control of their public schools.

☐ While the local school board enjoys the confidence of the people it
represents, it is still a human institution and, thus, there is room for
improvement.

☐ Local school boards—and their state and national associations—
have the capacity within themselves to cause improvement of the
local school board as a visionary, responsive, and sensitive educational governing authority in those specific areas identified in the
IEL report. All they need is the will.

This report should be read by everyone concerned about how
things actually get done in school districts.

For citizens, it emphasizes the importance of participating in
the democratic processes leading to the selection of school board
members—supporting candidates and holding them fully accountable
for their trusteeship.

For governors, state legislators, and state education officials, it
suggests the political fact that improvement in the instructional program, to be truly effective, needs the support of the people in the local
communities. Those people look to their local school board for leadership in this task. Therefore, state efforts to improve education must
involve school boards as an integral part of the process.

For school board members, it recommends critical areas of self-
improvement and self-evaluation of school boards.

And for state school boards associations and NSBA, it provides
a solid base on which sound in-service education programs for school
board members can be designed and conducted.

IEL—and its funding source, the American Can Company
Foundation—have done education, and therefore the future of the
United States, a real service through the publication of this report.

Nellie C. Weil, President
Thomas A. Shannon, Executive Director
The National School Boards Association
Washington, D.C.
October, 1986

Preface

Made possible through some well-placed dollars from the American Can Foundation, this report throws sudden and welcome light on that dark island of American governance, the institution that everyone knows of but few understand: the school board.

For those anxious to fine-tune this time-honored, pervasive American institution, the Institute for Educational Leadership provides immensely helpful guidelines. Based on new, in-depth surveys of school board practices and leadership across the country, there are careful reviews of school board training, of board functions, staffing, and how boards secure evaluation of their own effectiveness. The reader learns how the boards do deal and might deal with superintendents. Reading this report, school board members will know how **their** board's methods of operation compare with counterparts all across the United States. They will know what satisfies, what dissatisfies board members elsewhere. They will be able to read a set of well-researched, well-thought out guidelines for how school boards can operate more effectively.

This is also a very timely document. It looks into the tough new issues surrounding the board's appropriate role—"trustee" for good management, or representative of the community (or some segment of the community). It is an issue made all the more relevant, indeed compelling, by the sharp rise in minority students as a share of the schools' enrollment, even while, as this report shows, the vast majorities of school board members are white, middle class and generally male. Yet the boards **are** changing in composition as the recognition grows, especially in minority circles, of school board election as stepping stone to a political career. How can the older trusteeship concept and the constituency-based, advocacy politics of these times coexist on school boards? The report offers few answers, but it does illuminate the quandry.

I found it compelling to read how much the public believes in the need for school boards, how much it remains attached to the concept of grassroots educational self-governance. But it was equally disturbing to note, from this report, that the same public evidences essential illiteracy about the actual role and activities of school boards. Moreover, the public turns out in appallingly thin numbers to vote for the school boards it otherwise believes to be so essential. We are left with the disturbing question: If the school boards' popular constituency misperceives their role and doesn't care enough to exercise its franchise in their selection, how fully or forcefully will the boards **ever** be able to function?

Against that background, we learn not surprisingly, that school board members feel excluded and ignored in the vast wave of 1980s school reform initiated and pushed forward by state governments. In one sense this is a classic "central versus the provinces" problem. It would be amazing if we did not hear that school board members detest hard-to-accommodate state policy shifts and mushrooming state mandates. The authors note, most appropriately, that the states' own initiatives can easily be stymied and come to naught in the absence of effective support at the local school board level.

What darkens the outlook for harmonious cooperation is that the states moved so aggressively in education precisely because they believed, correctly or not, that local school establishments were **not** providing high-quality education. Clearly, the political, business and civic leadership groups of states across the country, the groups which congealed in extraordinary fashion to push through the reforms of the '80s, concluded that the school boards were failing to move effectively on such issues as rigorous student achievement tests, teacher assessment, and remaking curriculums to create a skilled future U.S. workforce.

A final, troublesome issue is raised by this report: That "local boards and their members have only sporadic interaction with general government and tend to be isolated from mainstream community political cultures." That might have meant little in a time of federal dominance in domestic policymaking, or when there was little public interest in educational priorities and policy. But, in the 1980s, when education tops the strategic planning concerns of many cities and counties, it could be a fatal flaw.

However timely and beneficial this report's practical proposals may be for the training, coordination and effectiveness of school boards, there remain these thorny practical and political questions. One would look for adventuresome, pro-active responses by the school boards: proposing for example that they participate collectively in extensive, frank exchanges on policy and budget problems with the general purpose government leaders, the mayors and councils and city managers of their communities. Such meetings should take place at least once a year, preferably more often. Retreats away from everyday pressure might be considered. Unless there is extensive dialogue and understanding, how can this vital function, the education of its youth and next generation, ever be integrated into a community's comprehensive planning?

Another potential step for school boards would be to delegate members to work cooperatively and intensively with the state governments in the next round of reforms, promised by the National Governors Association in August 1986, just before publication of this report. The governors proposed placing seriously underperforming school districts in a form of state receivership. They suggested permitting families to chose which schools their children should attend, and to allow high school students to attend public colleges during their junior and senior years, in effect introducing competition into a public education system which has rarely offered much consumer choice.

It is understandable that the education establishment perceives such proposals with deep misgivings. But the public may endorse the new ideas with enthusiasm. The question of the coming years may be: Where **do** the school boards stand? As much as their own principals, teachers and students, the boards themselves may face uncomfortably severe tests.

Neal R. Peirce
Contributing Editor
The National Journal
September 26, 1986

Executive Summary

After a long history of fulfilling the nation's traditional commitment to local, democratic decision-making, public school boards need help.

Evidence of problems has been accumulating—low voter turn-out for school board elections, public perception in many communities that controversy dominates school board decision-making and reluctance of civically qualified leaders to serve on school boards. A more recent, and startling piece of evidence is the almost total exclusion of school boards from state policymaking to reform education and indifference to their crucial role in the various national reports on education.

What has happened?

With a grant from the American Can Company Foundation, the Institute for Educational Leadership assembled a team of investigators with extensive experience in school board leadership and/or training issues to conduct case studies in nine major metropolitan areas, interviewing a cross-section of the leadership in each community. The study also analyzed responses to questionnaires from more than 200 school board chairpersons in these metropolitan areas and three dominantly rural states and reviewed the limited recent literature available on school board governance.

From these sources, the study team concludes that the American public strongly supports the concept of local governance of education through the school board, but this support does not necessarily extend to the school board in their own community. Despite the public's approval of local governance, it knows very little about the roles and functions of school boards. The dramatic increase in states' visibility in educational leadership creates further confusion about the responsibilities of school boards.

This adherence to an ideal—but apathy toward it in practice—bodes even greater trouble for school boards in the future. As student populations become more diverse and management more complex, local governance needs more informed support from communities, not less.

Other major findings include:

☐ School boards must take the initiative in improving their policy-making capabilities

☐ School board leadership should focus on improving education for all students and reconfigure board members' agendas

☐ School boards are not linked to general government agencies and are isolated often from community power structures

☐ School board members are seriously concerned about state-level intrusiveness but have not yet developed a strong response that would make them partners in education improvement

☐ The public holds school boards to a greater evidence of ability and commitment than other officeholders

☐ Board members must accept and deal with tensions inherent in their service—relationships with the superintendent, balancing of diverse interests within a community and conducting sensitive business in the open

☐ School boards recognize the need for their own development, but the resources and systems to provide this are inadequate

☐ Too few school boards conduct evaluations of their performance, and very few involve the "outside" in such evaluations

While school boards are quite aware of and attempting to respond to the demand for accountability from the public, boards tend to interpret these increasing demands as accountability for school district and student performance. Very rarely do boards see this as applying to their own performance in policymaking, and their behavior as a corporate body.

There are indicators of an effective board, gleaned from this study and from other investigations. This study and other investigations found that an effective board:

☐ Addresses most of its time and energy to education and educational outcomes

☐ Believes that advocacy for all students is its primary responsibility

☐ Concentrates on goals and uses strategic planning to accomplish them

☐ Works to ensure an adequate flow of resources and equity in their distribution

☐ Uses the strengths of diversity represented on the school board and in the community to obtain the enunciated goals for the system and fosters both assertiveness and cooperation

☐ Deals with controversy openly

☐ Leads the community in setting goals for education and encourages many forms of community participation

☐ Exercises continuing oversight of education programs, acquiring the background and knowledge to ask the right questions

☐ Works out the division of responsibilities with the superintendent

☐ Determines the mission and agenda of board committees, if they are used, and makes sure they coordinate with policy and oversight functions

☐ Establishes policy to govern its own policymaking and oversight responsibilities

☐ Invests in its own development

☐ Establishes procedures for selecting and evaluating the superintendent and for evaluating itself

☐ Collaborates with other school board leadership to influence state policymaking and funding

☐ Understands the role of the media and develops procedures for media contacts that do not manipulate media attention for personal gain

This framework for school board effectiveness is an agenda for action—action boards can take to improve their leadership role, and subsequently to create a more informed and supportive citizenry.

1

INTRODUCTION

"The board is made up of basically good intentioned people, but they don't have the experience or backgrounds to deal with complex issues."

Community leader,
Indiana

Local school boards provide Americans with grass roots leadership for public elementary and secondary education. States and localities charge school boards with this governance role. Yet boards largely have been ignored by both policymakers and the authors of independent studies in the unprecedented public discussion, debate and action around public education in the past five years. School boards must play their crucial role. To do so, however, they must be strengthened.

The Institute for Educational Leadership (IEL), with a grant from the American Can Company Foundation, recently undertook a study of local school boards to assess their strengths and weaknesses. The project is consistent with IEL's 22-year history of efforts to improve educational policymaking and the capacities of leaders in education. An independent, non-profit organization in Washington, D.C., IEL now has programs and projects devoted to this purpose in more than 40 states and localities.

The more recent national reports, such as the Committee for Economic Development's *Investing in Our Children,* the Carnegie Forum on Education and the Economy's report, *A Nation Prepared: Teachers for the 21st Century,* and the National Governors Association's *Time for Results: The Governors' 1991 Report on Education,* have stressed grass roots improvement of education. Thus, the time is appropriate to study school boards and to analyze their current capacity for leadership and policymaking in an era of increasing state education initiatives.

The project staff consisted of three members of IEL's core senior staff—Michael D. Usdan, Jacqueline P. Danzberger, and Barbara A. McCloud—all of whom are former members and presidents of school boards. Danzberger is also a former president of a state association of boards of education.

Project senior staff members included Luvern L. Cunningham, professor in the Department of Educational Policy and Leadership in the College of Education, Ohio State University; Lila N. Carol, a senior research associate at the Mershon Center, Ohio State University; and Michael W. Kirst, Chairperson of Administration and Policy Analysis in the School of Education at Stanford University. Carol is a former school board member and president, and she and Cunningham have worked extensively with school board members throughout the country. Kirst is a former president of the California State Board of Education and an influential participant in and analyst of the reform movement in that state and nationally.

IEL looks forward to sharing these findings with school boards and the associations that represent them, educators, and others in the policy community concerned with the important issue of educational governance and citizens.

Background and Methodology

On the basis of the many national and state reports on public education in the past few years, many initiatives are being taken with little or no attention paid to the local school board. Despite all the interest in "partnerships" between the business sector and education, raising student achievement, improving staffs, elevating standards, and changing structures, serious institutional bottlenecks are possible in many communities if school boards are uninformed and uninvolved.

Many school boards, of course, work positively for educational quality and improvement and have structured their operations to accomplish this. In other communities, board members do not share common visions for their school districts, and similar dissonance appears between superintendents and boards. Infighting, public airing of disagreements and an inability of boards and superintendents to work together and respond to diverse constituencies permeate many school system environments, particularly in urban areas. Unsatisfactory relationships, either between a board and its superintendent or among board members themselves, destroy a sense of mission for schools. Dissension causes confusion, affects the morale and professionalism of those who staff the schools and causes lack of confidence in educational leadership within a community. Eventually, it limits the education of children.

At a time when growing state influence and, indeed, prescriptiveness is affecting areas such as curriculum, teacher certification, teacher and student competency testing, and data collection, it is important to analyze and strengthen the capacity of local boards for local leadership and for a partnership role in the state policymaking process. Perhaps the role of local boards needs to be redefined or the spectrum of responsibilities reconsidered. Certainly a greater public understanding of local / state relationships and roles in the shaping of school policy is required, particularly now when the opportunity for change is so possible. Efforts to strengthen local governance can capitalize on the unprecedented interest in education improvement on the part of political, civic and business leaders at all levels.

The school board in American culture is truly unique. Its history of accomplishment spans more than two centuries. It is a singular institution in terms of both national and world experience. Problems of some magnitude, however, are emerging with regard to the role and operations of boards. Recent, in-depth research is lacking. Some descriptive accounts of the work of boards and superintendents can be found in the literature, but there is no recent solid data base upon which to generate recommendations for change in either this relationship or the role, functions and operating structures of boards themselves. This project was commissioned to help fill the void.

Information was gathered and analyzed on the structure, role and functions of school boards through several different methods, which provided a diversified data base. These included case studies in nine geographically and demographically diverse communities and a survey questionnaire mailed to 450 board chairpersons in these nine Standard Metropolitan Areas. Fifty board chairpersons in small rural districts in three additional states (Idaho, Iowa and Wyoming) also received questionnaires. Larger school systems with enrollments of at least 10,000 were selected for case studies. While systems of this size represent only 4 percent or 620 of the nation's school districts, they enroll 43 percent of the students. The project team also reviewed literature pertinent to school district governance.

Although this sampling does not cover the universe of 15,350 school systems and 95,000 board members, we are convinced that important commonalities exist, particularly in metropolitan areas. The study reveals issues pertaining to the structure and role of boards in general, but also cuts across urban, rural/small town and suburban districts. Similarities are more common than differences.

Granted, whatever one says about American schools and school boards is both true and false, depending upon where one looks. But recent national reports and the issues which they illuminate—student and teacher testing, desegregation, finance, the intolerable high school dropout rate, college admissions, collective bargaining, and relationships with constituencies and the media—create common *national* concerns that envelop school boards, despite the legal decentralization of our education "system" and ostensible local autonomy to determine policy and priorities.

The governance and management of local school districts are varied and complex. Further, the politically subtle forces that impinge upon governance and management do not yield easily to survey methods, particularly in volatile metropolitan environments. Understanding of these forces can be acquired better through in-depth interviews and observations.

Therefore, team members (at least two of whom visited each of the nine case study districts) used qualitative, participatory methods. The interviews were structured to allow cross-site comparisons while capturing the uniqueness and dynamics of individual districts. The teams interviewed several groups of local leadership—present and past school board members, superintendents and their top staffs, especially those who interact frequently with school board members. Interviewees also included business and civic leaders, the heads of major unions, media representatives, leaders of municipal government, parents, students and other citizens influential in the district and community. The interviews, in other words, were at the "grass roots."

The nine metropolitan areas on which the study focused were (with the case study location in parenthesis): Atlanta, Ga. (Atlanta); Columbus, Ohio (Columbus); Dallas-Ft. Worth, Texas (Lewisville); Denver, Colo. (Jefferson County); Hartford, Conn. (Hartford); Indianapolis, Ind. (Indianapolis); Pittsburgh, Pa. (Pittsburgh); San Francisco-Oakland, Calif. (Oakland); and Washington, D.C. (Alexandria, Va.). Although, as indicated earlier, the case studies were done in districts with at least 10,000 students, most of the data derived from the questionnaires came from much smaller districts located in the nine metropolitan areas and rural states. The data base thus includes smaller, more typical districts, as well as the larger ones in the case studies.

Characteristics / Demographics

For the past eight years, Virginia Institute of Technology and the *American School Board Journal* have surveyed a representative national sample of school board members. The profile from that survey[1] reflected the responses of 1,468 board members—from a random sample of 4,095 who were mailed a two-part questionnaire in February 1985. Survey results represent approximately 10 percent of the school boards.

Table 1, derived from responses to this survey, reflects the major concerns of board members and presents a personal profile, including information on sex, racial background, age and economic status[2]. As the data show, financial support issues are by far the most pressing concern of board members, with declining enrollment, collective bargaining, lack of parental interest and management/leadership issues clustered considerably behind. Concerns about issues of collective bargaining and management/leadership seem to be growing. In 1984, only 9 percent of the board members responding to a similar survey cited the collective bargaining issue, while in 1985 the percentage soared to 29.3 percent. Concerns about management/leadership issues were reported by only 4.7 percent of the board members in 1984; this dramatically increased to 25.7 percent in 1985.[3]

Board Members' Concerns   Table 1 (A)

Concerns	Percent*
Lack of financial support	54.6
Declining enrollment	33.7
Collective bargaining	29.3
Parents' lack of interest	27.5
Management/leadership	25.7
Finding good teachers	20.3
Use of drugs	15.9
Teachers' lack of interest	13.1
Disrespect for students/teachers	8.9
Overcrowding	8.9
Lack of discipline	8.4
Poor curriculum/standards	8.1
Pupils' lack of interest/truancy	7.2
Integration/busing	2.9
Crime/vandalism	2.2
Other	
Teacher relations	5.4
State mandates	5.0
Curriculum development	3.5
Facilities	3.5

Sex

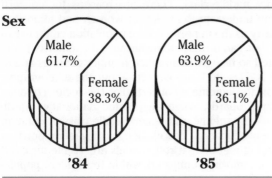

Ethnic**

Ethnic**	'84	'85
Black	2.4	3.0
White	90.4	93.5
Hispanic	1.5	1.2
American Indian	.8	.8
Oriental	.5	.3
Other	4.3	1.2

Age

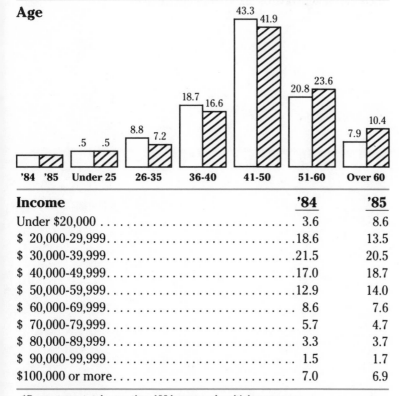

Income	'84	'85
Under $20,000	3.6	8.6
$ 20,000-29,999	18.6	13.5
$ 30,000-39,999	21.5	20.5
$ 40,000-49,999	17.0	18.7
$ 50,000-59,999	12.9	14.0
$ 60,000-69,999	8.6	7.6
$ 70,000-79,999	5.7	4.7
$ 80,000-89,999	3.3	3.7
$ 90,000-99,999	1.5	1.7
$100,000 or more	7.0	6.9

*Percentages total more than 100 because of multiple responses.

**Some percentages do not total 100 because of rounding.

The national socio-economic data reflect the fact that board members are solidly middle class. There are reasons for concern about the continuing underrepresentation of women and minorities on boards, particularly as the minority school population continues to burgeon[4]. National data can be misleading because the minority population is concentrated so heavily in a limited number of states and in larger urban districts. Despite these caveats about the demographic data, there is reason for legitimate concern that the socio-economic composition of school boards, when aggregated nationally, inordinately reflects a majority middle and upper middle class orientation for local governance of education. This challenges the assumption that special needs are being met or that role models are visible for ever-increasing cohorts of minority youngsters within the student population.

Responses to IEL's survey questionnaire and the information from case study interviews proved remarkably consistent with the *Journal* demographic findings. Data about school districts from our survey correlate closely with the national proportion of urban, suburban, and small town / rural school districts.

The IEL questionnaire to 500 board chairpersons had a return rate of 43 percent (216 boards). The sample represents 1,350 board members. Table 2 displays some of the information about school districts and school boards taken from our sample.

School District Characteristics   Table 2

Self-Description	Percent of Sample
Urban	11.0
Suburban	54.0
Small Town / Rural	35.0

Student Enrollment	Percent of Sample
5,000 and under	74.0
5,000–35,000	2.0
36,000 plus	24.0

Households with Children in the Public Schools	Percent of Sample
10% or less	.4
11–30%	49.0
31–50%	36.0
Over 50%	14.6

Economically Disadvantaged Students (determined by AFDC, state welfare, subsidized school lunches)	Percent of Sample
Less than 15%	68.0
15%–20%	17.0
21%–and above	15.0

Enrollment Increase / Decrease	Percent of Sample
Elementary	
Stable	20.9
Declining	30.4
Increasing	48.7
Junior High / Middle Schools*	
Stable	21.4
Declining	51.7
Increasing	24.3
High Schools*	
Stable	18.5
Declining	49.2
Increasing	23.9

*Percent does not total 100 because not all respondents answered this question.

School District Characteristics (cont.)   Table 2

Racial / Ethnic Student Population Changes

	Percent of Sample
Change in excess of 10% in past five years	
Yes	.9
No	68.3
Change of 10% or more projected in next five years	
Yes	.9
No	90.1

School Board Characteristics   Table 2

	Percent of Sample
Number of members on the board	
5	36.0
7	35.0
9	33.0
All Other	6.0

Male / Female Member Ratios

	Percent of Sample
5 member boards (74 in sample)	
Male	62.2
Female	37.8
7 member boards (46 in sample)	
Male	65.0
Female	35.0
9 member boards (68 in sample)	
Male	63.0
Female	37.0

Elected / Appointed to Board

	Percent of Sample
Elected	95.0
Appointed	5.0

Of the elected boards, 81% are elected district-wide

Term of Office

	Percent of Sample
2 years	4.0
3 years	23.5
4 years	68.3
5 years	0
6 years	4.0

School Board Characteristics (cont.)　Table 2

Average Tenure of Members	Percent of Sample
1–3 years	10.0
4–8 years	82.0
8 years plus	8.0

Board Member Education (1,350 board members in sample)	Percent of Sample
College degree	71.3
Some college	14.3
High school	12.4
Less than 12 years	0.5
Unknown	2.7

Compensation for Board Members	Percent of Sample
Yes	30.2
No	69.8

Race / Ethnicity of Members	Percent of Sample
White	94.5
Black	3.6
Hispanic	1.2
Other	.7

Age of Members*	Percent of Sample
Student	1.3
20–30	2.7
31–40	25.0
41–50	47.0
51–60	18.8
Over 60	7.2

Policy to Allow Employment of Board Members' Families	Percent of Sample
Yes	67.3
No	32.7

Are Family Members Currently Employed by School District?	Percent of Sample
Yes	62.3
No	37.7

*Totals more than 100% of sample

2
MAJOR
FINDINGS

"Americans love boards of education—but rarely their own."

A study team member

1. There is strong support for maintaining the basic institutional role and structure of the school board.

School boards are in trouble. As a grass roots institution, they confront a basic paradox. While the study found strong support among community leaders, parents, local citizens and educators for preserving school boards to keep schools close to the people, there concurrently was widespread public ignorance of their established roles and functions. There appears to be deep public apathy and indifference, as reflected in the difficulty of attracting quality candidates to serve as board members in many communities and in the abysmally low voter turnout for board elections. This civic ignorance bodes even greater trouble for school boards in the future, as student populations become more diverse and creative leadership more necessary. Systematic efforts to promote greater understanding of the important role of school boards must be initiated in communities throughout the country.

2. Despite basic support for maintaining the institutional structure of school boards, they can and must strengthen their effectiveness.

More time should be spent on educational issues and less time on administrative responsibilities and what the public perceives as "trivial" matters.

3. Boards must become more active and must exercise leadership for education rather than operate solely on the basis either of administrative or individual agendas.

Boards must build stronger links to other sectors of society and to the body politic. As elected (or politically appointed) lay officials, board members fail to capitalize as fully as they might on their electoral base and potential political influence. Too often boards are perceived as reactive rather than deliberative.

4. Board members increasingly are perceived as representing special interests, and the trusteeship notion of service in which board members represent the entire community has been less prominent in recent years.

Board members, educators and the public said that divisiveness and the problem of building a cohesive board from disparate members, many with single constituencies or issues, are major factors affecting board effectiveness and community perceptions.

5. Boards, particularly in urban areas, have become more representative of the diversity in their communities and often include indigenous leaders from disparate constituencies within the larger community.

This is positive in terms of diverse populations gaining access to board service. However, when board members are not from traditional community leadership and power structures, they lack easy and influential access to civic, political and economic decision-makers.

6. Local boards and their members have only sporadic interaction with general government and tend to be isolated from mainstream community political structures.

There is very little systematic communication between school system governance and general government, despite the fact that increasing numbers of students have learning problems associated with non-school factors. These include poor housing, lack of family support and resources and limited employment opportunities. In addition, when interaction between the school system and general government does exist, it often is only through the superintendent. Fiscally dependent boards which must interact with town/municipal government bodies frequently are mired in adversarial relationships. Some urban community leaders believe it may be time to rethink the non-partisan nature of school board elections. Perhaps election to the board through the mainstream political party structures is an issue worthy of debate in some communities. The majority of boards in the United States are non-partisan.

7. Board members are seriously concerned about the growing intrusiveness of the states as the reform movement evolves.

If they are to maintain public support, schools must remain responsive at the local level. When the authority of local education officials is transcended by state bureaucracies, schools lose their grass roots political support base. Local school boards are essential mechanisms of representative democracy. They deal with the most volatile and sensitive issues that effect the citizenry—namely, their children and their tax dollars. They would like to become recognized and effective partners in state dialogues.

8. The public appears to have a different set of expectations for the political behavior, degree of sophistication and level of general learning of school board members in contrast to other political officeholders.

This phenomenon may stem from the fact that at some level in the public mind there is a mystique about education. Whatever the reasons, the public (citizens and leaders) expresses high expectations about the performance of board members but often does not see them as community leaders. Yet the IEL survey found board members were twice as likely to have a college education as the general population.

9. Board members continue to grapple with tensions over necessarily gray areas between a board's policymaking and the superintendent's administrative responsibilities.

In the districts in which board-superintendent relationships are good, little attention is paid to this dichotomy. However, some school boards, particularly in larger heterogeneous districts, have or wish they could have staff serving board members directly. There appears to be less willingness in these districts to rely on the superintendent and administrators to "staff" the board.

10. The need for school board education and development is recognized generally, but too often it is merely informational and episodic.

There is minimal access to or involvement in developmental skills-building. Too little attention is given to development of working relationships among board members and to development of boards as corporate bodies. Boards which recognize the need for board development have retreats and goal-setting meetings, evaluate their performance and provide for oversight of the implementation of their policies. Such boards appear to have a greater sense of effectiveness.

11. Urban, suburban, rural and small town boards alike find more commonalities than differences among the challenges to their effectiveness. These include:

☐ Public apathy

☐ Lack of public understanding of the role of boards

☐ Poor relationships with state policymakers

☐ Need for board strategies to evaluate board effectiveness

☐ Lack of time and operating structures to focus on education

☐ Problems in becoming a board rather than a collection of individuals

☐ Improving teaching in the framework of collective bargaining

☐ The amount of time boards invest in their work versus satisfaction with accomplishments and ability to determine their own priorities

12. Board members in many districts are worried about long-range demographic trends which will cause changes in the composition of the school population and the voting public.

The decreasing number of families with school-age children may lead to an erosion of political support for the schools as the population ages and becomes more concerned with issues such as social security and medicare. Simultaneously, urban areas see an increase in the number of children with special needs. A concomitant concern is that more and more middle class parents, both minority and majority, will pull their children out of the public schools. This would further shrink the influence of the political constituency which has historically supported quality public education, underscoring the need to encourage the business community to sustain its recent interest in and commitment to the schools.

13. The majority of boards do not formally evaluate their own performance.

Demands for more accountability are increasing for all societal institutions—and school boards are no exception. Being accountable through voter decisions every few years no longer is a viable argument against regular annual board assessment of its performance against stated objectives formulated in response to student needs and community expectations.

However, in the IEL study only one-third of the boards had any structured self-evaluation. Among those boards that do evaluate themselves, there is no evidence of incorporating input from parents, the school system or the broader community.

3
A
TRADITION
IN
SOCIETY

"...public school is a most vital civic institution for the preservation of a democratic system of government" and the primary instrument for transmitting "the values on which our society rests."

United States Supreme Court
Abingdon School District v. Schemp
Ambach v. Norwick
as cited in *Statecraft as Soulcraft* by George F. Will

School board membership is the highest form of public service. It should be sought, not shunned; revered, not reviled.

Anyone who examines the American education system must be impressed by its size and complexity, yet local governance provides citizens a unique opportunity for involvement.

The local school board is the only means through which the community expresses itself in respect to education. Boards are the interpreters and translators of need and demand. They mediate between and among conflicting interests. They sort out contending values, and they initiate and enact policies to govern locally. Boards must do so within existing state and federal statutory boundaries that specify certain responsibilities and determine the limits of the boards' discretion.

In most of the nine case study districts, community leaders, especially those from business and other units of local government, emphasized the importance of education to the larger community. They were specific about the link between good schools and the local economy, the significance of a well-prepared work force in attracting industry, the contribution of full employment to quality of life, the role that schools can and must play in citizenship development and in meeting civic responsibilities. These attitudes are further substantiated in the August 1986 national survey by the Carnegie Forum on Education and the Economy.[5]

The role of the board as observed in this study is not just an artifact of the 1980s. It is the product of over two centuries of evolution, changing very little in terms of legal responsibilities in the past 75 years. School boards filter, interpret and translate the education goals of the people into a mission for the school district. Ideally, the composition of a school board would encompass the spectrum of individual and collective interests within school districts. Obviously, the heterogeneity of most communities makes the achievement of that ideal difficult, if not impossible. Nevertheless, board members are expected to be sensitive to the spectrum of community educational perspectives and expectations. They also are expected to somehow divine community consensus and provide leadership for that consensus.

Lay responsibility for public education is a cherished American tradition. Early on, American leaders distinguished educational governance from general local government. They saw it as special, and they lodged responsibilities with small groups of citizens. Although they are variously titled (school committees, school boards, boards of school directors, trustees, or commissioners) these lay persons are responsible essentially for the same education governance responsibilities, district by district, state by state.

The origins of lay control lie in New England, specifically in Massachusetts. The town meeting and representative government through selectmen took shape in Massachusetts and spread throughout the colonies. As populations grew, the tasks of governing education outstripped the time and capacities of local selectmen. Even though subcommittees of selectmen were assigned to oversee schools, the need for special attention to schooling was apparent. This led to local school districts and school committees as the structures for educational governance in New England.

The separation of educational governance from general local government was not achieved without struggle. The Illinois General Assembly in 1872, after a protracted period of controversy, separated the governance and management of the Chicago schools from the Common Council of the city of Chicago. Similar separation did not occur in San Francisco until 1917. Even now, there are varying degrees of dependency and interdependency existing between local school districts and other units of local government.

When Control Was Complete

In the beginning school boards were in complete control. They administered the schools on a day-to-day basis. They levied and collected taxes, hired and supervised teachers, provided school buildings, saw to heating and cleaning after a fashion, gave examinations to pupils (and occasionally to teachers) and certified children's progress so they could move from grade to grade. Board members reaped whatever political benefits came from patronage and controlling the tax rate, and although unpaid, they found enough satisfaction in this form of public service to seek and retain such responsibilities year after year.

School boards ran the schools until the 1830s when the first superintendents of schools were appointed. Decisions to employ full-time superintendents were made reluctantly, even tentatively. Occasionally, the decisions to hire superintendents were reversed after a few months or years, returning management to the boards. Growth in size and complexity eventually made it impossible for part-time boards to run the schools. Thus the practice of hiring superintendents became widespread, first among cities and eventually at the county level where superintendents administered many smaller, often rural districts of the county, each with its own board.

The encroachment of board members (currently often cited as a problem) on the day-to-day management of school systems is based on a long standing tension between governance and management. It is not new. The evolution of the board/superintendent relationship described in detail later on in this report is important. It is worth noting here that the quality of this relationship affects the overall effectiveness of a district's schools.

The work of a school board, as it plays itself out daily in a given school district, is a melange. The role is defined in large measure by state constitutional and statutory provisions which frame both the mandatory and discretionary aspects of a board's responsibilities. Court decisions, attorney generals' opinions, and rules and regulations of state boards of education circumscribe their work further. The expectations of individual board members, relationships with teachers and other employee groups, traditions of the district, the strength of the superintendent, education and other issues engaging the district at any given time affect the role. Voter behavior influences it, too. So do the educational expectations of interested citizens, especially parents. The media plays a part, at national, state and local levels. Consequently, the role is neither simple nor one-dimensional.

Findings on the Board Role and Function

Much of the IEL data reinforce conventional perspectives in respect to boards, and their roles and functions, but some do not. Data gathered through the survey of board chairpersons tend to support traditional views of boards and boardsmanship. Interview data, more detailed in many respects, provide new insights about the everyday life of being board members, the travail as well as the satisfactions.

One of the findings from case study interviews is the almost universal belief that school boards are important. They have serious public service to render, and a free democratic society cannot do without them. There is far less agreement and understanding, however, about how their function is to be fulfilled, or even what that function is.

School Board Role is Not Well Known

School boards are not very visible, in a general sense, nor in many communities is their basic function well understood. Boards seem to be taken for granted. No one wants to do away with them, but at the same time few people, even community leaders, know much about them, nor do they have many suggestions about how to improve them.

Some citizens believe that school board members operate the schools, are paid handsome salaries for doing so, and if something is wrong, a board member can fix it. This is far from the truth. These opinions show little sense of the board as a collective nor an understanding of a board's policy responsibility. Consequently, citizens contact individual board members, even cultivate them, make their interests known, and then expect board members to respond to their concerns as individuals. Such persons do not understand that a board member has no authority as an individual and can only bring problems to the attention of school personnel for resolution, or ultimately, perhaps, to the full board.

This attitude feeds a representative ideology for school boards. A representative-oriented board member often takes the constituent's demands either directly into the system personally or to the board as a whole. This conflicts with trustee-oriented board members or many school administrators who expect board members to respect the corporate tradition of boardsmanship. Such behavior also can result in divisiveness among board members if several are pushing for disparate interests or demands. The situation is often exacerbated in districts where board members are either elected or appointed by geographic areas within the community.

Most districts harbor a diverse "flow of images" about school boards. These are built over time through media coverage especially, but also through other forms of contact or association with the work of the schools. A good image is hard to earn and takes a long time to build. Over several decades, a district's board can experience several changes in its public image as a consequence of many factors. Declines can be tied to citizen beliefs that the schools are bad, or that there is too much conflict within the board or that the board fails to face up to difficult decisions. Unfortunately, subsequent boards may have to live with these perceptions. Few lay people have a grasp of what serving on a school board is all about.

School board members, past and present, said repeatedly they had no idea of how big a job it was to serve on a board. Many said that they were disillusioned when they learned how little authority they had and how difficult it was to get anything done. Clearly, the general citizenry is not informed about the role and function of school boards and, ironically, detailed knowledge of what boards do is missing as well among professional educators, especially teachers.

To be fair, districts vary in how well informed citizens are about their school boards. In at least one of the nine case study districts, the teachers, principals, business people, local government officials, civil rights leaders and other community leaders were well informed about their school board, knew the members by name and were able to compare and contrast the present board with previous ones. Moreover, they gave the current board high marks for its effectiveness.

Ideological Tensions

Two ideological orientations appear within school boards, as indicated by interview data—representativeness and trusteeship. Some board members see themselves as representing either a specific geographical area, or the interests of a narrowly defined group, or both. Others see themselves as general trustees of the public interest; they rely on superintendents and other administrators to run the district.

Those who hold the representative point of view are much like those who ran school districts before professional administrators were hired. They are not reluctant to interfere in management, nor to pass judgment on individual or system performance. They brandish the word "accountability" with abandon, usually in the name of this or that constituency. They do not view the system as a whole. Rather, they see a shabby school, an upset parent, a poor teacher, an unfair principal, an incident, a leaky roof, each of which is an occasion for intervention. However, board members who hold the special constituency representative point of view have frequently led the charge and caused redress of inequities and inadequacies in school systems.

Those who favor trusteeship see themselves as monitors or overseers, relying on the superintendent and other managers to operate the system. Such board members value managerial efficiency, allowing superintendents to develop the board agenda, report on the district's progress and recommend policy for board consideration and adoption. They place importance on hiring a top executive and holding that person accountable. Their decisions view the school district as one unit. The model is adopted from business and higher education. Its presence in school boards is the direct result of a powerful reform movement of the 1890s and early 1900s led by a coalition of university presidents and business leaders.

Incredible diversity (and complexity) confronts school boards in the 1980s. At times it seems overwhelming, beyond the capacities of board members to manage, even to comprehend. There are competing issues, competing philosophies, resource problems, turnover in board membership and/or administrators, state mandates, special interests, litigiousness, escalating expectations, enrollment growth and decline, personnel problems, demographic changes, lack of public confidence, competition from private education and uncertainty engendered by high technology. Such wide-ranging problems and issues make planning extremely difficult. There is neither time nor energy for commitment to planning, at least very far into the future. Surviving day-to-day consumes most of many districts' managerial and policy resources.

Business leaders interviewed recalled earlier times when they had served on school boards, along with what they called other "real" community leaders. Now, you can't get higher echelon business people to serve on boards, or if they do, they don't stay long because they don't want to put up with the hassle. By hassle, business people mean the constant harassment from parents, taxpayers, teachers' organizations, civil rights groups, and other special interests of many stripes, and the negative media representation of board actions. They become discouraged over the inability of the board to "get its act together." They become impatient, too, with the difficulties of managing schools and measuring productivity. After a while, these persons throw up their hands and leave, or become passive toward obstacles which they have been unable to overcome.

Racial and ethnic minority board members often feel the same way but for different reasons. Their frustrations turn, too, on the inability to get anything done. They chafe at bureaucracy, seeing volumes of rules and regulations as roadblocks to their own effectiveness as board members as well as inhibitors of quality education for minority students. They often feel strong ties to minority or ethnic constituencies and they believe those loyalties to be very important, more compelling than an abstract concept of ties to the district at large.

Other board members identify with specific program interests—reading, special education, vocational/technical education, athletics or a program for the gifted and talented. Occasionally, these are the only interests board members have, and they pursue them relentlessly without concern for other programs or district needs. Such persons often make judgments about programs and personnel on the basis of personal data gathering in visits to schools.

Consequently, there may be sitting at the same board table persons disenchanted over ineffective and insufficient procedures for getting things done, those unhappy because they feel minority children are the objects of discrimination and those who have special programmatic interests to push. These perspectives, of course, are not always consistent with what others in the community, including the professionals, think are important. In the absence of any mechanism to manage such diversity, school systems flounder and the educational welfare of children and youth are placed at risk.

What is needed is a way to manage diversity, rise above the idiosyncratic preferences of individual board members and chart a course for the district that transcends individual interests of board members but also respects them.

Leadership Can't be Dodged

Although many school board members chafe under federal and state mandates that encroach on local control, there is still an awesome leadership task for school boards. Technically, school board members are agents of the state, or extensions of state government to meet local needs. Responsibility for education rests with the state, not with local school districts. Ultimate accountability resides far from the schools themselves. Yet communities in this study strongly cherished the concept of local control through the school board.

Federal and state laws are quite specific about what local boards are to do. School desegregation is a good example. Many boards have devoted thousands of hours, often reluctantly, to shaping compliance with the U.S. Constitution in race and other equity matters. Courts at all levels, the Congress, state legislatures, state departments of education and other local government units impose their will on local boards, limiting local discretion. These sources spell out matters such as setting school district boundaries, transportation, finance, personnel, pupil attendance, pupil safety and health, school calendars, property acquisition and management, employing and firing of a superintendent, labor relations, minimum standards and, increasingly, many aspects of the curriculum. The one area where school boards in this study believe they spend too much time is in responding to state mandates.

Many board members, early in their tenure, are surprised at the scope of their legal duties as well as their specificity. Yet despite the size of the mandated work load, considerable room and responsibility for leadership remain. Local boards have leeway in determining the means through which to respond to mandates. There is freedom to adapt curriculum to local needs, especially in response to changes in pupil population and community goals. Boards can assess the impact of high technology and other external events upon the schools and school districts. Developing oversight policy rests with school boards, very little of which has been done to date. And boards could systematically produce policy to help them be better board members, but few do. Much remains to be done if grass roots leadership is to use effectively the latitude it has in local governance. The working board must know itself better.

4

THE
WORKING
BOARD

"There always seems to be additional information that causes us to change our minds."

School board member,
California

Time is of the essence. For school boards structuring time—its quantity, quality and focus—is the major challenge to effective and satisfactory operations. Through the questionnaire and site visit interviews, the IEL study probed how board members view their use of time and how representative community leaders perceive this issue. There is a clear convergence of opinion on the importance of this issue. But, opinions about the problems, as one might expect, differ.

Board members and chairpersons, with few exceptions, are concerned about the small proportion of time spent on "real" education issues. Yet board members, on the whole, feel they must do it all. One experienced board member said, "We can't give up any area, but the board is overwhelmed; we go from crisis to crisis; we can't find time for planning, and we don't spend nearly enough time on curriculum, teaching and student learning." However, one school board in a large district views itself, and is viewed by its public, as "a well-oiled machine." This is the exception.

One question in the IEL survey (Table 3) asked board chairpersons what they considered the three most important areas among 12 major school board policy roles. Thirty-nine percent indicated that *appraising curriculum* is one of the most important board functions. Yet 42 percent said the board spends too little time on this role.

Time on and Importance of Policy Roles * Table 3

	Too Little Time	Right Amount of Time	Too Much Time	Importance to Board
Defining and advocating for students' education and related needs	53	133	0	84
Setting standards and adopting policies for personnel selection, evaluation and professional development	49	134	4	61
Appraising curriculum in terms of district's needs, goals and objectives	84	100	2	77
Continuous goal setting, policy development and appraisal for the system	80	105	3	60
Raising community aspirations for educational excellence	84	96	6	23
Working for school system and community focus on access and equity for students	29	150	5	13
Providing visible leadership for public education in the community	44	143	1	34

*Numbers in each column represent the number of responses to each.

Time on and Importance of Policy Roles* *(cont.)*   Table 3

	Too Little Time	Right Amount of Time	Too Much Time	Importance to Board
Maintaining system and community focus on student achievement and improving student achievement	51	133	3	45
Expanding the number and types of constituencies that support and participate actively the public education	86	94	6	9
Providing leadership for financial support of the school system and allocation of resources to support the district's goals and objectives	32	146	10	80
Capitalizing on the national education reform momentum and initiating reforms appropriate to local needs and goals	44	134	10	10
Translating state legislation and regulations for local needs and goals	32	129	25	17
Other (please specify)	1	3	9	1

*Numbers in each column represent the number of responses to each.

Thirty-one percent checked *continuous goal setting, policy development and appraisal for the system.* Forty-one percent believe their board spends too little time on this policy role.

Boards view themselves, and are viewed by even critical publics, as "well meaning" (this was heard over and over) and composed of persons trying to do a good job. But the scope of a board's responsibilities, except in its legal terms, seems to defy definition and structure and is planted with unexpected landmines. Board members are politicians (93 percent of our sample are elected). Constituents (personal, system, other political bodies) are major forces in defining the job and the priorities—and frequently contribute to the crises. Despite all the time spent responding to local crises, constituent (and staff) issues, and media criticisms, what does the external world say? "The board doesn't spend time planning, thinking, setting priorities for its policy work, and assessing the system's education." Or, "This board is really into crisis management." Indeed, board chairpersons (50 percent of the sample) said the key step their boards could take to strengthen policymaking and leadership would be to engage in more study sessions and policy review. Sixty-eight percent of the sample said their boards have regular goal setting/planning meetings—but almost one-third of the sample do not.

The answer is **not** that boards should spend more time. Actually, some boards may need to decrease the hours spent. Board work should concentrate on the policymaking function—setting priorities, defining goals and objectives and assessing achievements against objectives. Boards must discipline themselves and educate the public to a board's effective use of its time. A board which structures its work within:

☐ Goal setting,

☐ Determining priorities to focus the board's work,

☐ Planning to achieve objectives,

☐ Utilizing structures for review and oversight of policies and board actions,

☐ Creating systems for effective internal and external communication (to and from the board), and

☐ Evaluating itself

increases both its own sense of effectiveness and positive perceptions among its constituencies. While the time a board spends may not be reduced, it will be better spent.

Developing and, more importantly, operating within such a structure requires management and interpersonal communications and leadership skills. Board members, former board members and community persons interviewed stated that, by and large, their boards of education, as corporate bodies, need development in these skills.

Board Operations

The study looked at how boards currently organize their internal board work, their working relationships with the school system and their relationships with various leadership groups in the community.

The sample was evenly divided between boards that have formal committees of the board and those that meet as a committee of the whole for all board work. Of those boards with committees, only one-half said the committees are formal and written into board operating policies.

Committees seem to work better for homogenous boards in smaller communities than for urban boards with racially, ethnically and politically diverse constituencies. This is consistent with the representative philosophy of board membership that has begun to dominate urban boards. Interviews with board members highlight trust (or lack of trust) among board members, constituents' lack of understanding of the role and authority of individual board members and a board member's definition of his/her individual role as issues affecting the willingness of board members to give up individual responsibility through a committee structure.

Oversight

Structures for oversight and monitoring board policies are glaringly absent. The exceptions occurred mainly for court-ordered actions, such as desegregation. Only 21 percent of the sample said that implementing and monitoring board policies absorb most of the board's time. In interviews with present and past board members, all stated that the oversight function is sorely neglected—again, the lack of time was cited.

The absence of visible board activity in oversight and policy monitoring affects a community's perception of the board. This ranges from appalling reactions in the business community to, "They pass a policy, but I never know what happens," among parents.

To meet their oversight responsibilities, boards could incorporate implementation plans with new policies. Such plans might include periodic reports back to the board from the superintendent. Another strategy would be to assign oversight of policies to board committees, which would report back to the full board on their defined areas of responsibility. **Neither of these suggestions requires more board time**. Board members cited over and over their frustrations in terms of accomplishments for the time spent. But, without a structure for assessing results of board action, it is difficult to have a sense of accomplishment.

Power of Information

Board access to information is critical to informed decision-making. The study revealed that where once boards may have felt this was a problem with superintendents or staff, information now is more abundantly and freely given. Indeed, superintendents spend a great deal of time "servicing" boards' information needs—in some instances almost to the point of overwhelming the board with information. Some observers, indeed, have expressed the suspicion that this is a deliberate administration strategy.

Where relationships are good between the superintendent and the board, there is an easy attitude about board members going to other staff for information. However, in these same districts, board members have the courtesy to inform the superintendent. Conversely, where there is lack of trust, individual board members frequently develop their own sources of information among staff and have been known to use such information to "blind side" the adminstration.

Information is power in any policymaking situation. How one gets it and uses it tests the integrity of individual board members and the operating practices of boards.

Board members need to weigh their perceived individual needs for information against the corporate board's need for and use of information. The person hours required of system staff to respond to requests of individual board members should be weighed against the board's corporate requests for information. If the board has priorities for its work, available staff time should be devoted to these priorities. The superintendent and board chairperson must educate and discipline board members and staff to the organizational policies. A corporate board policy for information requests from the system requires the self-discipline of individual board members, not only with respect to staff but also in relationships with constituents. Don't, in other words, promise information that must be delivered through procedures contrary to board policy.

Results of interviews with citizens suggest that board members, despite their adequate and organized information systems, are perceived to be making many decisions on the basis of anecdotal information. It is difficult for officeholders to avoid the known anecdote as a rationale for decisions or political positions. However, the public expects that decisionmaking in education will be based on solid, neutral information and will display a substantive knowledge of the issues.

Evaluation

Only 33 percent of the sample boards have policies for formal self-evaluation. In a political climate where demands for accountability are increasing, boards are beginning, however, to see the need for such a policy. There was no evidence of board self-evaluations that formally include the staff or community.

Board self-evaluations which included such constituencies could narrow the gap between a board's sense of its effectiveness and the public's perceptions. For example, a board self-evaluation at the close of the school year with input from the "outside" would allow the board to review its priorities and plans for the year, assess achievements, and deduce problems. This process could encourage the board, school system and community to develop a set of common expectations for the work and performance of the board.

Staffing the Board

Increasingly, boards in large systems within politically complex communities are establishing staff positions assigned to the board. These "board offices" range from one person for all to a staff person for each board member in the "mega-cities." Board members appear to be sharply divided on this issue. Generally, boards which are more homogeneous in communities which are less diverse oppose the concept of separate board staff. Yet many cities have board staff, and in cities where this is not the case, some board members are pushing to establish such positions.

As with so many issues, this one probably has no right or wrong answer. The sheer volume of work for boards in large districts would seem to support the concept of board staff. However, having their own staff allows board members to become much more involved in day-to-day activities in a school system. A we/they split between system staff and board staff can develop, as well as tensions with the superintendent. Like so many situations, it can work well if the people trust each other and if the motives of board members do not include creating a power base parallel to the superintendent or the system.

Role of the Board Chairperson / President

Board members and citizens alike believe the board chairperson is critical in determining whether a board is effective or ineffective. A good chairperson is fair, allows all points of view to be heard, and prevents any individual on the board or in the audience from "hogging the show."

Board chairpersons are viewed by their fellow board members as "first among equals." The study produced little evidence of dominating, autocratic styles among chairpersons. The board leadership role has evolved into facilitating the work of the board and building consensus.

Board members as well as community members look to the chairperson to manage board "mavericks" and to prevent the "three-ring circus" perception on the part of staff and community.

There was general acquiesence, if not full agreement, among board members that the chairperson plays a critical role as a sounding board or lightning rod for the superintendent in anticipating board members' attitudes, reactions and probable actions in regard to superintendent and staff initiatives.

Board chairpersons in the study appear to have, at a minimum, considerable board experience and knowledge of their communities. Seventy-eight percent in the sample had served on their boards four or more years, 78 percent had college or postgraduate degrees, 79 percent were over 40 years old and 93 percent have lived in their communities 10 or more years.

Operating Within the School System

The most common type of formal board / staff relationship is that of staff assigned to work with board committees. Sixty-six percent of the sample boards with established committees have specific staff assigned to committees.

Obviously, informal relationships develop among board members and staff. These relationships can add to trust and the board's sense of security about what is happening in the system. Board members need to be sensitive to the fact that staff members report through the system to the superintendent—staff can be "whip sawed" between board members and those to whom staff reports. This is viewed as dysfunctional by all parties. It is very difficult for a staff person to say "no" to a board member who wants information or a task performed. Staff persons, according to the site interviews, will rarely tell a board member the cost in time and neglected duties required to respond to his or her request.

Relationships with the "Outside"

Municipal / town government: School boards too often are isolated from general government, and, except in the small percentage of school districts where boards are elected through political parties, they are isolated from mainstream political party structures. The study found no regular structures for relationships with other governmental bodies except in those cases where boards are fiscally dependent—and these relationships tend to be adversarial.

Interviews in the site visit communities revealed major concerns about the absence of structured regular communications. This situation:

☐ Allows municipal government to distance itself from the school system and problems of the board

☐ Isolates the board from political power structures
☐ Creates frustrations among community leaders about a lack of coherent community planning with respect to financial resources, human resources development and economic development, coordination of bond issues and other problems

Interviews in the case study districts indicated that where there is regular communication, it occurs through the superintendent.

Media: Generally the board chairperson is the spokesperson for the board with the media. The superintendent is perceived as spokesperson for the school system. This is a fine distinction that somehow seemed to sort itself out in most systems in the sample. Board members are least tolerant of a colleague who seeks media opportunities to display opposition to full board action. Citizens, particularly local leadership persons, also view this behavior as destructive and evidence of political immaturity.

Constructive board/media relationships are most difficult in highly political environments where board members represent distinct constituencies and must deal frequently with inflammatory issues. Larger school systems frequently have an office of communications or public relations and, to the extent possible, boards rely on these professionals for day-to-day communications with the media.

Business: Regular interaction with business leadership occurs most frequently in communities where board members come from the historic "elites"—once common for board members. In such communities, board members themselves are frequently on the boards of the local Chamber of Commerce, Rotary, Lions and other civic and cultural organizations. These are informal but productive relationships which provide links for the board as a whole to community power structures.

Boards, **per se**, rarely have formal structures for relating to business leadership. However, more and more superintendents have taken the lead and established relationships with the business community. A superintendent's initiative in this area of district/community relations can confront school boards with both organizational and personal challenges to their board leadership role.

5

GETTING ALONG
WITH THE
SUPERINTENDENT

"My job is to help them learn to become effective... I will not shy away from telling them when they're dipping into administration."

Superintendent,
Non-harmonious district

Some school boards go through cycles. School districts have had periods when boards and board members earned high marks from community constituencies. Those who served on such boards were esteemed and respected for their insight, integrity and understanding of the school board's role and that of the superintendent. They were able to distinguish between what an individual board member is to do and what the board is to do as a collective. But changes in board membership occur, boards can drift into other patterns of behavior, less constructive and threatening to past board achievements. Boards may lose public confidence and find themselves unable to develop a common bond sufficiently strong to carry them through the difficult decisions they must make.

Those interviewed for the IEL study frequently referred to former boards or individual board members. Examples of unity and common purpose were cited and persons were singled out who had given exemplary service on the board. They commented as well about the significant role the chairperson plays.

The subject of administration/policy interaction is hardly a new topic in education or in other governance contexts. It has been analyzed and described over and over again. Yet it is still difficult and often misunderstood. It is an axiom that administrators should stay out of policy and that board members should refrain from intervening in administrative affairs. In the day-to-day welter of governance and management, however, those lines become blurred. Some critics maintain that where there is encroachment in either direction difficulties arise. Others believe board members can participate substantially in the administrative activities of a district without harm, and that administrators may cross into the policy domain without undue negative consequences. Absolute separation of responsibilities is misleading. There can be settings and conditions, for example, where violation of the rule produces positive results.

In the case studies, we found typical examples of positive and negative encroachment:

1. A strong superintendent, trusted by board members and instilling confidence in community leaders, violates the textbook definition of separation of policy and administrative functions, but the situation appears to work satisfactorily. This was the situation in one large urban district in the study where board members were not uneasy about the central role the superintendent plays in policy development. In fact, the media, community and parent representatives viewed the board members as "leaders" because they created a team with the superintendent. He, however, was given credit for "providing the glue." Because board members gave the superintendent a free rein and backed him publicly, they too were perceived as strong leaders.

2. The opposite of this situation is one where the board encroaches upon the superintendent's domain. The case studies yielded one of these examples, too. At this site, the board members take active and sustained interest in the management of the schools, from the central office to the building level. The board's interest in personnel decisions smacks of patronage. The stance of this board has

become fixed in the public's mind. One of the citizen's interviewed commented that "the board is about the same as it has been over the years—very much into administration."

This kind of enroachment leads to policy initiatives originating with individual board members rather than with the board as a whole or with the cooperation of the superintendent. It also leads to short tenure for superintendents, as was true for the school district in this case study.

3. A third type of enroachment is a mixture—board and superintendent cross over into each other's domain. Often it is hard to determine where policy initiatives originate. However, both the board and superintendent can find this arrangement satisfactory—when all parties understand and agree that it should be this way. It works only when the board and superintendent have confidence in each other.

In the case study that typified this style, the superintendent is a political leader among influential community groups; board members acquiesce to this so long as he keeps them informed. The board sees itself as the "boss," but observers note that the board initiates little in major policies. However, board members feel they "must be involved in everything and know what is happening day-to-day in the system."

4. Finally, there is the textbook definition of separation of roles. Everyone understands and accepts the idea that policy and management are different functions, and the board and superintendent do not intrude on each other's responsibilities. Each participant knows what is expected and abides by those understandings.

In the case study which illustrates this model, the board's role was described as one of letting the people know "what is happening—a citizen watching over professionals." The board honors cooperation within itself, deplores confrontation with the superintendent—but sees itself as the entity that must ask the important questions about the schools for the public.

In communicating policy and actions, the board tends to give the "why," while the superintendent gives the "what and when." The board works as a team through "good committee work." The superintendent follows up immediately on policy development with the leadership staff and teachers.

Hiring, Evaluating, Firing

The most important single task of a board is to hire a superintendent. When asked what their biggest job is, board members will say usually that it is the employment of the superintendent, evaluating this person and firing the individual if he or she does not measure up to the district's needs. When there is a vacancy in the superintendent's position, board members invest a long time in a search process. Boards frequently employ consultants, involve the community and the professional staff in the process and then look for assurance that they selected the best person.

Usually, there are good reasons for a change in the superin-

chief executives. Often there is rapid turnover in the boards themselves, and each new board wants its own person. There are a few districts in the United States that are concurrently paying off several contracts of previous superintendents. Buyouts do not contribute to good school community relations, as many districts are discovering.

Thus it behooves every board to concentrate heavily on the search for a superintendent and to specify clearly the conditions of employment, including how the person is to be evaluated. Once those are in place, the board and the new executive should live by what has been agreed upon.

Evaluation of the superintendent—and of the board—is serious business. In the districts surveyed, about 90 percent formally evaluate the superintendent, yet only one-third of the boards indicated procedures in place for board evaluation, most often through a self-evaluation process. The small percentage of board members who did not believe in evaluation of board performance argued that such evaluations are handled at the ballot box. State school boards associations have refined methods and procedures for superintendent and board evaluations. Some of these are very sophisticated and helpful, but much remains to be done to improve the appraisal of governance and management of local school districts (see Chapter 8).

At the time of turnover in the superintendency, boards need to be aware of potential transition problems. Often an interim superintendent is appointed or there is an extended lame-duck period following a resignation or firing. Long periods of time without a chief executive can create problems which lie in wait for a new superintendent. Board members often cannot resist the temptation to get in and "run things." Central staff sometimes are without direction or possibly have too many directions. Boards need to see that governance and management of the district do not drift during the transition.

The time of the superintendent's appointment is the time to clarify roles and responsibilities. Each of the issues below, confirmed as potential problems in the survey, offers the board and the superintendent the chance to clarify views and begin afresh.

Board Member Relationships with Other Employees

Ideally, individual board member contacts with other employees of the district should be cleared through the superintendent's office. However, the governance and management of school districts rarely reaches the ideal, and it is not possible for superintendents to hear all requests to meet with, or otherwise contact, district employees. Also, often board members have been active in parent/teacher organizations and have established friendships, patterns of communication, even social acquaintances that continue.

Further, habits of friendship that may be nourished during the transition period between superintendencies are hard to give up when the new executive arrives. Other patterns of communication and dependency develop when central office staff are assigned to work with board committees. Boards rely heavily upon such persons for information, even direction, for their committee work. Board members develop impressions about central office staff through committee work, and staff often see it as their opportunity to influence the board directly. Thus, superintendents unintentionally can be removed from some critical daily governance and managerial activities.

Information and Information Flow

Producing, providing access to and sharing of data often are serious issues. Board members comment about receiving too much information, not enough, or information that in their judgment is inadequate or unreliable for their purposes. Further, not all board members want the same information. Some superintendents then are confronted with a dilemma: do they provide their boards with less information, more, the same amount or data of a different kind? Too much information was a common complaint with some boards in the interviews.

When board members feel they are ill-informed by the superintendent or central staff, they may seek additional data elsewhere. Such "searches" often result in serious problems. Superintendents feel threatened by board members who use the organization on a day-to-day basis for information. Similarly, board members feel frustrated when data do not appear to answer the questions they have.

Equity in information access is another issue in many school districts. Some board members believe they do not have the same information as other members. Occasionally, they are concerned that individual board members appear to have the "ear" of the superintendent, call that office frequently or meet with the chief executive independent of other board members.

It is important that board members, the superintendent and the staff clearly understand the information climate, clarify it and develop guidelines.

Agenda Development and Control

The survey results indicated that board chairpersons and superintendents jointly develop board meeting agendas. In a few instances, the board itself developed the agenda, and in about 20 percent of the districts surveyed superintendents developed the agenda by themselves. (A 1982 survey of school superintendents showed them to have a much larger role in board agenda development than was true in this study.)[6] This is an important area. Those who control agendas define problems and issues that will receive local district attention. Differences in the findings between the school boards and superintendents could be the result of "in-the-eye-of-the-beholder" phenomena.

Serving the Policy Needs of the Board

In most of the case study districts, superintendents reported spending considerable time serving the policymaking needs of the board, as much as 85 percent in one instance. Much of the literature, until recently at least, focused on the superintendent's managerial duties, not on helping board members. The precise responsibilities of superintendents for policy development (the primary board function) have been treated sparsely, both in research and in preparation programs for administrators.

This function includes helping the board develop a policy calendar, delegating specific staff help to the board for policies under consideration, offering consultation on matters where the superintendent has particular expertise, expediting policy deliberations and assisting the board with the final policy statements. After a board has adopted policy, responsibility for implementing it is firmly with the chief executive. Policy oversight, notable in its absence in the boards surveyed, is the board's domain but requires the superintendent and executive staff to gather data for evaluation of implementation of policies.

Competition for Headlines

Boards and/or individual members of the board frequently compete with the superintendent for public attention. This may be more widespread in larger districts, but wherever it occurs, it is serious.

Some board members precipitate the problem because of their political ambitions or wish, at the least, for re-election or re-appointment to the board. Others resent a superintendent always seen on TV or quoted by the press. This seems to occur, according to the survey and case studies, even when board members admire and respect their superintendent.

Consequently, the issue becomes how to share properly in both the applause for a job well done and the criticism which inevitably accompanies both policy and administrative responsibilities in education. It is important to recognize this problem and to address the issue directly. Written board policies for relations with the media can help. These should be developed after open, frank discussion with the superintendent about his/her role with the media vis-a-vis the board. Board members should also work out among themselves members' relationship with the media—is the chair the board spokesperson? If other members are approached to appear on TV, radio or comment for the press, do they clear this with the chair? Are the politics of the community such that it is important for all board members to have some media visibility? Superintendents should be sensitive to the visibility needs of board members who are politically elected or appointed. Board members who can effectively relate to the media can be an enormous asset for the school system in relating to the community.

Importance of Trust

Those interviewed for this study, especially board members and superintendents, emphasized the importance of trust. Asked to cite the key strength in working with their superintendents, board members often cited "openness in communication" and "trust/confidence/support " (Table 4). The major problems of working with the superintendent were too much board involvement in administrative matters, a lack of board freedom and independence and too much for boards to do without adequate information. These findings are central to trust. Findings of the IEL study are supported by a survey of school board/superintendent relations sponsored by the National School Boards Association and the American Association of School Administrators in spring 1986. In this survey trust and respect were highlighted as major reasons for good relationships.[7]

School boards and superintendents need to address these areas of potential problems—and of potential harmonious relationships—if they both are to respond adequately to the issues facing them.

Working with the Superintendent   Table 4

Major Strengths	**Number of respondents answering question**
Trust/confidence/support	64
Openness in communication	75
All Other	51

Major Problems	**Number of respondents answering question**
Lack of board independence	11
Board too involved in administrative matters	17
Too much to do/too much information	13
Superintendent seeks to resolve issues too quickly	6
All Other	79

6

ISSUES

CONFRONTING

BOARDS

*"From our perspective, the
major issue is the state effort to
usurp local control and make
school districts holding
companies for the state."*

Board member,
Colorado

Board members feel responsible for too many "very important" issues. They feel the pressure of traditional issues dealing with student performance, efficient management, proper staffing, and financing. Within each of these issues are nuances that further challenge board leadership.

However, the survey and case study interviews revealed (See Table 5), often for the first time, new issues dealing with such problems as state-level political interference with local decision-making and public apathy (and sometimes antipathy) toward the role of school boards. These have been evident before in many communities, but they emerged as strong themes in this study.

Program issues mentioned most frequently were the need to:

☐ provide more flexibility for the diverse requirements and learning styles of an increasingly pluralistic student population

☐ improve the high school completion rate

☐ improve the transition to employment

☐ improve the academic achievement of at-risk students

☐ maintain a balanced curriculum in which an appropriate mix of traditional academic and job-related instruction is provided

☐ increase early childhood programs so that the schools' focus can be on prevention rather than remediation

☐ pursue equity while maintaining high academic standards

Teacher and Administrator concerns were:

☐ The challenge to ensure high teacher quality, with the demographics working against such an effort

☐ The need for stronger building-level input and leadership in the development of educational programs

☐ The need to improve staff development

☐ An impending teacher shortage

☐ Competency testing for teachers to screen out ineffective individuals

☐ Career ladders and merit pay as a way to make education financially attractive and more competitive with business and industry

Leadership and management issues which concern boards included:

☐ The impact of state student and teacher testing programs

☐ The potential effect of inter-district comparisons of student achievement

☐ Political status and influence of school boards

☐ The need for independent sources of information

☐ Financial crunches from unexpected pressures, such as higher insurance rates

☐ Negative perceptions of the board stemming from open conflicts and constituent pressures

A major, common issue confronting school boards is the problem of attracting and keeping high-quality teachers. Boards are also concerned about weeding out poorly performing individuals and raising mediocre performance of staff. Although concerns involve administrators as well, the spotlight has been upon teachers, as reflected in the recent *American School Board Journal* survey mentioned earlier.

As may be expected, school boards must deal, usually through teacher unions, with teacher questions about board policy on such issues, which opens up a veritable Pandora's box of concerns expressed in negotiations, and contract administration. The 1985 *American School Board Journal* survey attested to the growing importance of collective bargaining issues at the local level. Since no real increase in states that mandate collective bargaining has taken place, this growing concern would seem to indicate that issues important to boards are increasingly affected by collective bargaining.

Education Issues for Boards
Policy Roles   Table 5

	Very Important	Increasing in Importance	Little Importance
Public pre-school education	18%	41%	41%
Special interventions for at-risk students	30%	55%	15%
Student high school completion	56%	19%	25%
Programs / strategies for persons who have dropped out of school	13%	40%	47%
Adult basic education	16%	27%	57%
Reform of vocational education	19%	46%	35%
Inservice staff training needs	55%	31%	.03%
State student testing programs	34%	53%	13%
Teacher testing programs	18%	52%	30%
Merit pay or other pay differential for staff	23%	44%	33%
Demands of special interest groups	10%	40%	50%
Impact of court decisions	34%	42%	24%
Changes in insurance companies' policies for public bodies	56%	30%	14%
Extended school day	14%	44%	42%
In-state comparison among local school districts of student achievement	23%	49%	28%

The IEL interviews yielded valuable information on board members' perceptions of political, demographic, governance and other major issues as well as their concerns about school programs. Most board members expressed particular frustration with the public's lack of knowledge and awareness of the structure, role and purposes of the local school board. They perceived a pronounced lack of support for and understanding of the significance and unique functions of boards in their communities, even among well educated and involved citizens. As a result, boards often lack the requisite political clout to improve the schools. Board elections are often marked by low voter turnout, high turnover rate among board members and lack of quality among candidates.

Obviously, a community which does not have a positive attitude about what is happening in its schools is unlikely to contribute the kind of support desired by the school system. The reported lack of parent commitment and/or interest and involvement in the schools may be, in part, a reflection of this poor image of public schools.

These trends do not augur well for the schools. They must compete politically for resources at a time of growing fiscal constraints. Many board members complained that more of their colleagues now represented special interest groups and that the trusteeship concept of representing the entire community had been weakened. Apparently, growing numbers of board members lack experience in group decision-making.

The lack of adequate financial support for schools is particularly vexing. This includes insufficient money for existing educational programs, facilities, and personnel, as well as a lack of money for changes or additions to the educational program. Closely connected to this is the frustration experienced by local boards as they try to respond to new state mandates unaccompanied by the money needed to develop and implement them.

Related to the lack of proper financial support is the decrease in the number of households with children in school. Many school boards are concerned about the changing characteristics of the taxpaying population in their communities—specifically, the increase in the number of elderly people and others who have no children in school. School boards are acutely aware of the need to broaden the base of their political constituency to assure necessary support for public education.

Apprehensions also were expressed about the decline in the number of board members coming up the volunteer pipeline from service in local PTAs, Leagues of Women Voters and other local groups. These well-educated, dedicated civic leaders are decreasing in number as more and more talented women pursue careers. A number of interviewees felt that the caliber of board members had declined because of the loss of such volunteer talent to school systems.

Most board members were quite concerned about the growing influence and intrusiveness of the states in local district affairs. They find the mushrooming of state mandates and the centralization of policymaking frustrating, and they feel impotent and powerless in the decision-making process. Some board members indicated they would not continue to devote the time if they became only administrative pass-through agents for policies devised in state capitals.

Board members also stressed changing student demographics as an issue of paramount importance. The school population increasingly is composed of minority youngsters who often come from economically disadvantaged backgrounds. Their parents generally lack influence in the community, and thus the political support for public education has been weakened. At the same time, many of the growing numbers of older, economically comfortable majority group citizens without children in the schools are more interested in social security, medicare and local tax rates than in supporting education. These demographic realities, as well as the loss of the middle class majority and minority students in many districts, create serious political problems for school boards. There is an acute need to broaden the base of political support for education.

Specifically, the interest and commitment of the business community must be sustained, particularly in some large core urban centers characterized by a sense of isolation and despair about the future of public education. In non-urban systems, particular apprehensions were expressed about the ripple impact of negative media attention to troubled city school systems. Metropolitan area populations, it was feared, might get a false perception from television, for example, that all school boards and school systems are permeated with incessant political conflict and controversy.

About Themselves

Board members generally agreed they lacked preparation for board service. In essence, many newly elected or appointed members felt totally unprepared for their new responsibilities and unaware of the inordinately large amount of time board membership entails. They expressed widespread support for more extensive and diverse training to make new members more knowledgeable and better equipped to discharge their responsibilities.

New board members, it was felt, should be exposed to large amounts of information. They should become more familiar with the organization and processes of school system operation and more aware of their unique role as members of a public governmental body. *All board members* should learn how to function in a corporate body and understand how decisions are made in a group policymaking context. They should continuously assess the ever-touchy realm of board-superintendent relationships and develop sensitivity to the nuances of what is policy and what is administration in the public school decision-making environment.

Board members need to seek information from a variety of sources and learn what questions to ask of staff. Boards need to concentrate on their policymaking and oversight roles and avoid getting bogged down in minutia and administrative duties. Time must be spent on current issues, but boards need also to structure their work to devote adequate attention to policy, planning and evaluation issues.

Big Foot: State Policy Initiatives

One element that is very different for current boards is the intensity and scope of recent state policy actions. The most striking feature of state/local relations in the last 20 years has been this growth in state control over education. Today, organizations of professional educators and local school boards are making suggestions for only marginal changes in proposed new state policies. And under the Reagan Administration, the federal role has been restricted to rhetoric, collecting data and sponsoring small pilot programs.

These trends are ceding considerably more control of education to the states. However, there will be enormous variation in how states take control—from the highly aggressive states, such as California and Texas, to the least, such as New Hampshire and Colorado.

Dangers attend aggressive, broad-based state education policy. States change policy through statutes and regulations, which have a standardizing effect. Moreover, the new focus of state policymaking is no longer on categorical groups, such as handicapped or minority students. Instead, it is aimed at the core of instructional policy, including what should be taught, how it should be taught and who should teach it.

In part, the states appear to be playing such a large role in instruction because of a lack of local initiative. In general, local school boards, administrators, teachers, parent/teacher organizations and taxpayers simply react to state policymaking. Perhaps these organizations lack the capacity for policy analysis that the states built between 1965 and 1980.

State-level political actors leading the current wave of reform are legislators, governors and business interests. The traditional education interest groups—teachers, administrators and school boards— have been used primarily in pro forma consultative roles.

It is noteworthy that the increasing state control of the past decade has not been limited to such traditionally high-control states as California and Florida. The high tide of state intervention in local instructional policy is also washing over Virginia and Connecticut— longtime bastions of local control.

National movements and widespread coverage in the media have played a crucial role in the current wave of reform, just as they did in school finance reform and in the minimum competency testing movement. The initiatives moved through the states without any federal mandate or organized interest group lobbying. Political leaders had discovered that more money for education, combined with reform, could be a winning campaign.

The recent spate of reports on the state of education nationwide indicates a loss of confidence in the ability of local authorities to provide high-quality education. Consequently, state legislatures have felt compelled to step in and preempt local discretion, and these actions have been directed at the heart of the instructional process. A major contention between many local boards and their state policymakers is that many of the reforms were initiated or enacted in local districts prior to state action.

What the Study Found

These overall trends in state policy are clearly evident in the field study and questionnaire. Indeed, there was a growing sense of alarm among local school boards about state intrusion. For example, 85 percent of local boards responded that they believe their state is becoming more directive overall. When asked if their boards, in the last two years, have devoted time on their agendas to education reform issues, 55 percent responded yes. Forty percent or more respondents listed these issues: increased graduation requirements, revised curricula, teacher evaluation / competency testing and student testing. Asked if the national reform movement has encouraged the board or community to initiate change, 44 percent responded yes. A majority reported that the state is becoming more directive and creates more local board agenda items.

Despite wide historical differences in state control traditions among the nine metropolitan areas and rural states in the study, state influence is growing in each state. Every school board is concerned about it but recognizes some substantial benefits (e.g., more dollars plus public support of quality education). Increased state influence is evident in terms of new areas for state policy focus (for example, curriculum and teacher evaluation). Every one of the states in the IEL sample has increased drastically its scope and intensity of state-mandated testing. The aggregate effect of recent state reform on teacher morale requires careful scrutiny, given the responses from Texas and Virginia that emphasize poor morale caused by the totality of recent state actions.

The trend in each state is toward more direct state influence rather than an emphasis on policies giving flexibility to local boards. The reforms are having a psychological impact on local board members in terms of their uneasiness about the future state role. There is evidence of an actual impact on local policies. This broad concern surprisingly was as intense in states with few initiatives (Colorado) as states with many (Texas).

What can be said about all this? First, it is part of a long-term trend. It has not "crippled" local school boards, but in California and Texas, for example, their ability to respond to local conditions has deteriorated, and the trend has produced many major agenda items— and much paperwork. Local boards cannot take the policy initiatives they could take 20 years ago. Moreover, state policy is not determined in significant part by local school board considerations. School boards associations are perceived by state policymakers as defensive and reactive to recent state initiatives, rather than as actors in setting the state agenda.

The range of recent state actions is very wide, making generalizations about system and school-level impact hazardous. But local boards seem to have no clear strategy to reverse this aggressive state policy trend. The incremental growth of state involvement, over time, is more significant than the 1983-86 spurt in state legislation, but boards do not understand why state authorities have lost confidence in them. Board agendas historically, however, have not displayed a major concern with issues that dominate the current state policy agenda:

1) teacher assessment, 2) curricular quality and coherence, 3) economic competition, and 4) enhancing school building leadership.

Board members complain that state policymakers ignore the aggregate and cumulative effect of their policies on state/local governance patterns. Various crises trigger quick state responses and mandates. Board members do see many positive benefits to pupils from state activity, but worry about their own prerogatives and, specifically, about the "leveling" effect of statewide policies on the better school districts. More research is needed as to why state school boards associations have limited effectiveness in shaping state policy initiation and implementation. Boards, too, are not alone in their uninvolvement in state reforms; superintendents also feel they have had a minimal part in the action.

State by State Differences

While the general pattern is clear, there are differences in local perspectives. In Virginia, for example, tension is growing because of state mandates for teacher evaluation conducted by the state and a concern that art, music and vocational education will receive too low a priority. Teachers' salary expectations have been raised by state reforms, but state money is not sufficient to begin to satisfy these expectations.

Ohio boards did not display as much state and local tension. State initiatives often reinforced policies adopted or actions taken locally prior to the enunciation of the statewide policies. On a relative scale, Ohio has not dramatically increased state involvement.

In Connecticut, the school boards, especially the urban boards, feel they are unable to get ahead of state initiatives and that they are simply reacting to state testing and curricular policies. The Connecticut State Board of Education is much more activist than in the past. The state has a high level of educational achievement and probably a disproportionate number of "lighthouse" districts. These suburban districts—and this is true for other such districts in all the states—have operated in the context of national standards of excellence among like districts. In these districts, states have not been perceived as guiding influences for excellence. The issue of confrontation between minimum state requirements and "lighthouse" school districts surfaced in Texas also.

In several states, school board members complained that state mandates help improve low quality local districts, but are not particularly helpful and even deleterious to the better districts. Some districts in the sample believe the state is forcing them to take steps backward—particularly in types of testing programs for students.

In sum, the state role is having a major impact on local school boards. It is ironic, however, that so little attention has been paid to school boards in the myriad of current national reports and state commissions. Why this national and state inattention to school boards during a period of intense education reform? Perhaps policymakers do not feel they know how to improve local school boards—or they do not think boards are a problem area. Perhaps among some there is the false assumption that mandated reforms can occur without local involvement and "ownership." Perhaps there is the arrogance of "we know best." Whatever the reasons, the state/local school board relationship deserves more sustained attention than it has received. This relationship also greatly affects school boards' perceptions of their own effectiveness.

7

—THE—
GOOD AND BAD

"We tear each other up..."

Board member,
large urban district

What are the satisfactions and dissatisfactions board members derive from their board service?

Almost half the respondents to the IEL questionnaire believed they were fulfilling their commitment to improving education in their communities. Almost half also found satisfaction in working cooperatively and harmoniously with other members to achieve common objectives. A substantial number of board members enjoyed the opportunity to meet diverse people and gain varied experiences in their communities, as well as in the wider realms of state and national policymaking.

Many of the board members in the case study districts gained satisfaction from discharging an important public and community service. Where board members work well together, serving on the board is an enriching experience in which an individual shares a sense of progress and pride, working with colleagues and staff to achieve mutual goals.

Service on a board of education also enables members to demonstrate leadership in areas in which they have particular expertise, such as finance, labor relations or architecture. Respondents also expressed satisfaction with their involvement in activities and processes where success is visible and mentioned increased staff accountability through more rigorous evaluation procedures, more parental involvement and improved student achievement. Some board members were pleased they could handle difficult issues like desegregation and school closings with rationality and courage, despite differences of opinion both within the board and in the larger community.

Board members also were pleased to be part of the education system at a time when schools are in the public limelight. Crucial issues such as the need to strengthen standards, improve minority achievement, and provide special services to the academically gifted and other special needs groups finally are receiving the public attention board members believe they long have merited.

Generally, the more things are going right, the more satisfying is board membership, as might be expected. Board members and the community as well feel positive about board leadership when: student achievement is up; relations with the press are good (coverage is "fair" and balanced); parent involvement is high; the superintendent and the staff respect the board, provide adequate and useful information and buy into its policymaking role; the board functions well in terms of its committees, its monitoring of policy implementation and its handling of controversial or special interest group pressures; and the chairperson gracefully maintains "fairness, openness and order."

Dissatisfactions

When these things aren't happening—even just one of them— dissatisfactions can become almost overwhelming. Those enumerated by board members ran the gamut, reflecting in part the myriad of sensitive issues which require board attention. Many boards and communities express their dissatisfactions comparatively—judging today's situation against how "old boards" performed.

The most common complaints from the survey were the

factionalism/individualism that frequently divides boards and the difficulty inexperienced board members have in working as part of a corporate body. Other weaknesses mentioned were the inexperience of so many board members and, concomitantly, board member frequent turnover, weak goal setting, poor communication and too much attention to detail.

According to the questionnaire data, board members are unhappy with the policymaking process in their districts. Many board members want to strengthen their policymaking but feel hindered by lack of adequate time, increasingly restrictive laws and policies and unclear definition of their policymaking role and how to distinguish it from that of the school administration. There is too little time to think about these issues.

Interviews with board members in the nine case study districts affirmed a number of these dissatisfactions:

☐ Many colleagues don't understand their role and how to operate in a large organization

☐ Many board members lack management/corporate experience and are oriented toward single-issue concerns, making them susceptible to the pressures of special interest groups

☐ The board lacks cohesion, and the members at times do not reflect a "trusteeship" concept of service that represents the entire community

☐ They lack independent sources of information and are dependent upon the superintendent, leading to a public perception that the board is "dominated" by the staff

☐ They must concern themselves with peripheral issues while neglecting those central to students and schools. Too much time is spent "putting out fires," many of which are fanned by conflict-interested media

As to forces and influences outside the school board, those interviewed criticized:

☐ The general public's indifference and lack of knowledge about the role and responsibilities of board members

☐ Embarrasingly low voter turnouts

☐ Difficulty in persuading qualified individuals to run for the school board

☐ "Unfair" comparisions of student performance in this country with students from other nations, particularly Japan, West Germany and the Soviet Union, reflecting a lack of understanding about the diversity of the student body in the United States

A number of members acknowledged the weakness of their boards in the areas of policy development and oversight. There is too little time to deal with real educational issues—the agendas are glutted with administrative items pertaining to mundane business matters. The real "gut" education issues are being slighted. For example, they spend massive amounts of money on remediation programs but rarely have the opportunity to discuss, as policymakers, the program and cost-benefit advantages of investing in preventive pre-school or early childhood programs.

Board members also expressed frustration about how slowly schools change and how difficult it is to break through rigid school bureaucracies. Some believe, in fact, that professional staffs sometimes plan to "outlast" more transient board members. Several experienced board members, cognizant of staff influence and acknowledging board oversight limitations, stated they would not adopt policies until they saw the regulations that would implement them.

Many board members were candid about their perceived lack of clout and how difficult it is for them to achieve measurable or tangible results. Their rewards for being board members are largely intangible. The satisfactions may be few. Sometimes board service becomes a liability, undermining the community status of board members, although in earlier periods board service conferred high community status.

As was discussed in the previous chapter, the issue of state encroachment on local educational decisionmaking is a major issue and concern of board members and is a major cause of current board frustrations. The recent spate of initiatives at the state level are regarded with ambivalence. On the one hand, efforts to raise teacher and student standards, increase funding for schools and broaden education's visibility and political base are viewed as positive. On the other hand, the growing centralization of authority by state officials is viewed critically. Many of the new state regulations and initiatives, for example, are considered intrusive and are allegedly a constraint on local flexibility or even, perhaps, counter to local goals. Many state mandates do not provide requisite resources at the local level to implement them. Some board members claim that state policy often is oriented to the lowest common denominator, ignoring local differences and special needs. Indeed, of all the issues which create dissatisfaction among board members in their *leadership* role, growing state intrusiveness and lack of local involvement with the state are particularly, and deeply, felt.

Communities Sound Off

The attitudes of communities toward their school boards reflect the same desire for harmony that boards experience. A community is satisfied when its board is "working as one entity" or when it reflects a "business-like image." A community likes its board to be involved with community leadership and to foster parent involvement as well as citizen input. A community holds its school board up to closer scrutiny in terms of sex and race balance than it does other local agencies. It also wants board members to have a genuine commitment to the welfare of children and to be planning wisely for their futures.

Communities do not like bickering, "grandstanding" school boards. Nor do they like well-intentioned but ill-prepared board members (those without the civic leadership skills necessary for board service). A community becomes frustrated with a board that is perceived as disorganized, "always flying from crisis to crisis," or a board that seems either entrenched in old ways or isolated from other community policymakers. Just as it often makes a comparison between an older board (the good guys) (or vice versa) and current board, a community, and indeed an entire metropolitan area, may believe that city boards are not so good as suburban boards. A community also is critical of a board which does not "sell" itself or its agenda to the public, as well as of individual board members who do not provide good role models for school board service.

8

BOARD

DEVELOPMENT
—LEARNING ON THE RUN—

*"We have board training, but the
ones who need it don't go."*

Board member,
administrator-dominated district

Effective boardsmanship is not automatic when an individual is seated as a school board member. With little orientation and less training, the new person is thrust (ceremoniously, in this case) into a decision-making role in an arena where the member probably has little knowledge or direct experience. It frequently comes as a shock to discover that having statutory authority doesn't make one a leader in the eyes of the public.

The role of a board member calls for the exercise of authority over a diverse range of topics including discipline hearings with legal ramifications, budgets allocating millions of dollars, campaigns for tax levies, employee negotiations, approval of textbooks, goal setting and oversight of operations and programs, to name a few. It is not unusual for a new board member, on the first day of service, to serve on a hearing panel in a drug-related disciplinary case, or to make a judgment on installation of a computerized system costing in the millions. Additionally, the board member has to become a part of a corporate body and must understand the difference between acting in an individual capacity and as a member of a board. While campaigning, most individuals stress their own ideology and anticipate their own action programs as board members.

Data from interviews with board members indicate that many initially were ignorant of the extent of information and skills required of them as board members. Many held beliefs about school boards that turned out to be unfounded. The new member tries to scan the new environment, absorbing as much as possible in order to become a fully functioning member immediately. For the most part, this is unrealistic unless the board member is given ongoing training. Only as board members begin to use their newly acquired authority do their needs for training and development become apparent to them and to those observing or working with them. Traditionally, new board members were seated and expected to listen and learn before venturing opinions or introducing new ideas. Today in some communities, particularly where board members are chosen by electoral districts and viewed as representatives of specific constituencies, there is little if any time to learn. They are thrust into active, often turbulent environments, making decisions immediately.

Beyond knowledge about school finance, contract administration, teacher tenure acts and the like, school board members must understand how to make decisions wisely in a group situation, particularly one which is so public and important. The conviction is growing that board members need to be part of a continuous program of education and development.

Current Developments

Several studies in recent years have focused on board development needs. An American Association of School Administrators 1982 study of the superintendency provides some information about how superintendents see the need for board development[8]. And in 1986 the Ohio State University survey of state school boards associations was helpful in assessing how and to what extent such organizations are responding to boards' and board members' needs[9].

The literature on school board development makes a distinction between activities for new members (referred to as orientation), and activities that involve all members at varying levels of board experience and tenure. Virtually all new board members have orientation opportunities through state school boards associations, state education departments or their own local districts. Taking advantage of these opportunities may remain the prerogative of the individual member or may be a group decision. In a 1978 study, 60 percent (149) of the respondents (in school districts of less than 10,000 students) reported that orientation and in-service training programs were conducted in their districts[10]. In a 1980 survey of board members in southwestern Michigan, nearly two-thirds of the 277 respondents had attended one or more inservice programs at the local level; one-half had attended one or more regional programs; and one-third had attended statewide programs[11]. These data describe all inservice training and are not specific about programs geared to new members.

Superintendents participating in the 1982 AASA survey (1,294 school districts) indicated that 95 percent provided new board member orientation. Forty-two percent were involved at the local level only. In the IEL survey, 81 percent (153) of school board chairpersons reported that an orientation program is provided for new members. However, 86 percent of the boards (162) have members participating in seminars, training programs and conferences (other than new-member orientation) provided to board members by the state departments of education and state school board associations.

Who has the responsibility for developing and conducting the orientation? Does the superintendent control the agenda and the direction of the orientation and thus influence the initial socialization experience of a new member? Data from the IEL study indicate that education professionals at district and state levels are the chief architects and providers of a new member's introduction to the world of board membership. This finding is corroborated by the AASA 1982 superintendents' study in which it was shown that the responsibility for developing and conducting an orientation program rested with the education professionals at the local and state level. In fewer than 5 percent of the districts do experienced board members take the responsibility.

Despite the assumed influence of the superintendent over board members, substantial data indicate that board members, particularly in urban districts with changing clients and cultures, are more strongly influenced by their constituencies than by the traditional school superintendent who is still overwhelmingly white and male and still likely to come from a rural or small town background.

Surprisingly, almost one-fifth of the school districts in the study do not provide orientation, and 16 percent do not participate in state-sponsored programs. Of these, more than one-half cite a lack of time as the reason. About one-fourth are not interested, and the remaining indicate a variety of reasons for not participating. On the other hand, board members do attend other conferences and programs concerned with education issues as well as problems of governance and management of education.

Programs sponsored by state school boards associations

account for most of the development activities attended by board members. They provide "boardsmanship" conferences ranging from new board member workshops held during election years to intensive training over several days. These are devoted to specific information on budgets, legal issues, collective bargaining and other duties assigned to boards. Workshops also are given on other topics related to personal problems in the school community, such as child abuse, chemical abuse or communicable diseases. Relationships affecting board operation often are agenda items. These include board-administrator relations, intra-board relationships, superintendent evaluation and conflict management. All states appear to provide board members with code-of-ethics materials. In training and development parlance, these activities described in the IEL survey and in the Ohio State University survey basically convey information, possibly develop knowledge, but do not build skills.

Leadership skills acquisition for board members apparently is not emphasized in most of the state associations' programs. While they are assuming leadership in board development, only a few state associations have full-time directors of board development. Where such positions do exist, these staff persons are usually responsible for developing training materials, providing technical and development services directly to boards, holding individual consultations with boards, providing some assistance in crisis management situations—and upon invitation—going into a district for "trouble shooting." As more states have become involved in educational reform, some innovative practices have been devised, ranging from requirements that all newly elected and appointed board members receive training to leadership academies with three-year cycles of volunteer training. Strong incentives are built into some of these programs.

In the IEL study, a substantial number of respondents (42%) noted that their boards in the past two or three years have used outside organizations or consultant services for board development. More than two-thirds (69%) reported that when they use external consultants for board development, the superintendent and senior administrators participate in the sessions. Twenty-six percent involve only the board and the superintendent, and 5 percent prefer to hold board development sessions without the superintendent.

The study of board chairperson agenda items yielded 80 topics for board development sessions. More than three-fourths of those (63) were related to board processes; far fewer (6) were related to teachers and teaching, two were concerned with curriculum, one related to students and the remaining 10 percent were spread across a variety of subjects.

Distinguishing between what is and what ought to be, board chairpersons enumerated 175 items as the most important areas for development programs. Thirty-eight percent (78 responses) highlighted help in developing more effective board operations (meetings, decision-making, organization). Next in importance was help in goal setting, followed by assistance in how they could make better personnel evaluations and how to help their members clearly understand the legal responsibilities of the board.

Thoughts About Board Development

Interestingly enough, few board chairpersons gave priority to the human elements inherent in functioning as an effective board. Relationships—among board members, between board and superintendent, other administrators, teaching staff and community—are more important in determining how a community perceives its board of education than are the policies which the board adopts. The ability to communicate with the community and the staff is crucial, but, how members of the board interact with each other influences the kind, quality and timeliness of their decisions. Further, the behavior of board members can have a profound influence on the degree of confidence a community has in its leadership.

As noted earlier, the philosophical orientation of board members varies considerably from the stereotype of 50 years ago, when most saw themselves as institutional trustees. Now greater numbers view themselves as representatives of some (or all) of the community rather than as trustees who rely simply on their own judgment for decisions. This individual orientation influences the interactions of the board and members' perceptions of the role of the superintendent and staff.

Consequently, each board really needs opportunities to engage in thoughtful discussion about the human relations aspects of a board's internal functioning, as well as opportunities to build and sustain improved skills in these aspects. Conscientious attention needs to be given to examining the quality and kinds of interactions among all members of boards, but few boards engage in such an examination, according to the study data.

The environment in which boards operate has been altered considerably by the open meeting laws of many states, known familiarly as "sunshine laws." Conducting the public's business in public affects the functioning of the board and staff, and the public's perceptions of their work. Learning to do business in the sunshine is difficult for some board members, but not for all. Twenty percent of responding chairpersons indicated that sunshine laws inhibit the work of their boards, while 16 percent said their work was enhanced; two-thirds indicated it had no effect. Those who saw no effect may be comfortable dealing with tough issues in open board meetings—or they may be saying that more and more issues are finding their way into executive session without public or media objections. Some boards may be ignoring the law. Interviews indicated that some board members develop their own capacities to deal publicly with controversial issues and, over time, see the value of openness. They even become comfortable with the public and media attention which flows from the law. For others, the sunshine requirement is threatening and too much to handle. Consequently, important problems may not be well reasoned or may be decided in the welter of emotional climates generated by controversial open meetings. The public nature of board meetings encourages some persons, both on the board and in the audience, to engage in "grandstanding" or politicking. An important aspect, then, of board development is training in the skills required to do the public's business in public.

New—and experienced—board members need to consider carefully individual board member relationships with the superintendent, central office staff, other professional and classified employees, students and the community (individual, agencies, and organizations). This should not end with new member orientation. Wholesome, productive board inter-relationships require a concerted, ongoing effort on the part of the entire membership, with all contributing their perceptions and sentiments about these relationships. Much of what new members have to learn should take place with other board members drawing heavily from their knowledge and experience. Board training sessions can be viewed as opportunities to review and reaffirm board members' commitments to school board service, to appraise current performance and plan for needed improvements.

Increasingly, boards are engaging in formal evaluation processes for their superintendents (88%). Far fewer boards, however, conduct a formal appraisal of their own performance (33%), nor do they give their chief executive officer the opportunity to provide them with feedback on board performance. Where boards and superintendents have a common understanding of what their respective roles are, it is not difficult to develop an agenda for positive feedback and an opportunity to conduct such sessions in a healthy environment.

Development of that "common understanding" of roles can be achieved in part by developing with the superintendent a shared vision of what the school system can become. Such sharing does not occur without careful planning and perseverance. It requires prior understanding of the importance of the district's mission and general agreement that board and staff need to join in a common effort to achieve goals. Moreover, it requires time for deliberation, time that is reserved to develop the mission and to clarify and define continuously the district's goals. Agreement on mission and goals cannot be taken for granted. Mission and goals are the proper backdrop for all board development activities.

Effective board development relates also to the time, continuity and consistency with which the development/training process is carried out. Boards with regular development programs plan for continuous growth. Most board development activities, however, are one-shot, single events. Development should be planned like any other learning activity, with specific objectives, opportunities to "practice" and evaluation of the outcomes. Not only should the substance give board members the information necessary to make specific decisions (e.g., finance, legal cases, special populations), but it also should relate to the processes and environment in which the board conducts its business.

How does a board best go about making its decisions? How do boards differentiate between the board's policymaking role and the superintendent's administrative responsibilities? What roles do individual members have in the organization? Neutral parties from outside the system can be helpful to boards especially in sensitive areas such as roles, responsibilities and relationships.

These aspects of boardsmanship arise within all boards but outside assistance usually is requested only when boards are experiencing internal problems or are in trouble with their communities or superintendents. A continuing program of board development is a necessary and desirable aspect of school board service.

Operating educational institutions has become and will continue to be far more complex than formerly, making the need for the combined leadership of the board and superintendent an integral prerequisite to success. Planning together, particularly for strategic planning that involves systematic study of trends and monitoring of change, can be a powerful instrument for leadership development for board and superintendent. New approaches to strategic planning allow leaders of public institutions to keep pace with change and adjust more rationally to events occurring near and far. School boards in the IEL study were accused and accused themselves of only reacting, usually in crisis situations, rather than looking ahead and planning for the future. Substantive training can put boards out in front. Lay leaders are not expected to possess the professional knowledge and skills of the educational field, but the lay school board must be an informed and skillful political body exercising leadership of the school system for the community.

9

BECOMING
AN
EFFECTIVE
BOARD

"We don't discuss education."

Board member,
Indiana

The findings of this and of other studies point to the need for a framework within which school boards and those concerned with their governance **function** can assess effectiveness and define areas of need for improved leadership performance.

Accountability has become part of the vernacular and the vigor of public agencies in contemporary governance, but school boards have tended to limit accountability to school district performance or voter preference in election years. There needs to be, as well, accountability of the function of school boards—their performance in policymaking and monitoring.

While there are clear implications for individual board members in the following indicators of effectiveness, their use should be to guide the board as an entity. It is the whole board, not individual members, that is charged with governing the local school district.

Indicators of an Effective Board

1. An effective board addresses most of its time and energy to education and educational outcomes.

Because their service is part-time and "voluntary," school board members must concentrate on those priorities most relevant to their function, and where their leadership is most needed in a community. Assuring hot rolls in the cafeteria probably is not so important as taking the time to educate leaders in the community about an important policy decision facing the school board. Granted, policies are less easy to frame than are practical solutions to managerial responsibilities, but school boards must accept the premise that policymaking is the job they must do.

An effective board, for example, will spend a substantial amount of time studying and developing specific policies on content of instruction, student performance standards, quality of the teaching force and the provision of effective instructional leadership by principals and supervisors. An effective board will use school-by-school data for its discussions and policymaking.

As a beginning:

☐ Analyze the use of time the board spends as a whole, separating managerial from education policy activities

☐ Conduct a community survey to determine what functions and policies of the board need to be communicated better and understood and what the community believes is being neglected

☐ Set aside time at each board meeting to learn about and discuss a specific education issue, concern, or activity of the school system

☐ At a minimum, schedule special quarterly policy meetings where the community has an opportunity to participate

2. An effective board believes that advocacy for the educational interests of children and youth is its primary responsibility.

Citizens want school boards to be aggressive advocates for children and youth, as well as watchdogs of the public purse. School boards are the only publicly designated stewards at the local level for the education of children and youth. They are charged with the educational welfare of all students, irrespective of age, sex, race, ethnicity or ability to learn—schools and society are paying for past defaults in this responsibility. In their advocacy roles, school boards should recognize the essential link between educational excellence and the economic and social health of communities.

As a beginning:

☐ Make advocacy a stated goal of your school board, with appropriate policies for board actions

☐ Analyze each policy initiative, in public discussion, in terms of what it will do for students

☐ Be the catalyst for community discussion and action on issues that affect the welfare of children and youth

3. An effective board concentrates on goals and uses strategic planning to accomplish its purposes.

Without comprehensive study and analysis based upon reliable information, school boards likely will drift, at the least, or be so buffeted by state directives or local special interest pressures that they will fail to discharge their responsibilities to the children and youth in their communities.

Strategic planning should serve both policy and administrative needs. The two should complement each other, using appropriate information sources and technologies. This requires an understanding of strategic planning and how to do it, as well as a clear sense of the resources available.

As a beginning:

☐ Acquire training in strategic planning and incorporate its elements in board policy guidelines

☐ Constantly monitor ways to use new technologies for planning, e.g., analysis of community survey data by computers

☐ Require, through board policy, that each new board member receive expert training in strategic planning

4. An effective board works to ensure an adequate flow of resources and achieves equity in their distribution.

If a school system depends heavily on local taxing resources, then community understanding, support and involvement in schools must be a primary goal of the school board in order to avoid crisis-oriented funding patterns or inadequate resources.

But there are further priorities concerning resources. A board's responsibilities extend also to concerns about equity among schools and among programs, e.g., providing proper balance for arts, physical education, vocational education, special education or remedial education. Lack of attention to this kind of equity can result in an imbalanced education program—and pressures from the community.

As a beginning:

☐ Structure public discussion of the school budget in terms of school district educational needs

☐ Ask for community advice, in a structured way, for choices that reflect needs balanced with resources

☐ Provide monitoring of resource distribution among schools and programs

☐ Lobby with other boards for adequate resources from the state level

5. An effective board harnesses the strengths in diversity, integrates special needs and interests into the goals of the system and fosters both assertiveness and cooperation.

Certainly, it is difficult for a school board to accommodate positively all the points of view represented among its members. It is an even greater challenge to channel that diversity in ways that strengthen the board and the community's perception of it. Board members need to discuss their differences and seek ways to compromise or develop new definitions around which most of the board members can unite. They should be open about differences, specify their nature and content and deal with them as items of concern. Diversity should be respected.

Unfortunately, some members enter board service with little or no experience in dealing with conflict or with public scrutiny of differing viewpoints. Without the personal skills to manage conflict situations, board members often back themselves and their positions into corners, making policy decisions difficult for them and even more so for the board as a whole.

School boards and individual school board members develop competencies through experience and with the support of focused board development. Both need to be aware that expertise in working together while respecting each others' views can be learned—but it does not come naturally to most people.

As a beginning:

☐ Make time for the board to receive training regularly in human relations skills, setting goals for itself in this area

☐ Monitor the diversity in the community, making sure that the board has information on such influences as new populations in the schools or changes in the economic health of the community and the effect those changes have on families

☐ Involve the diversity of the community through policymaking structures, such as advisory committees and task forces

6. An effective board deals openly and straightforwardly with controversy.

Controversy is not new to school boards. However, the current scenario perhaps is more diverse and, at times, more strident than in the past. Public interest in the curriculum ranges from controversy over creationism to pressure for more science and math education. School closings and site selections generate public heat; a community's values often must be explored while selecting, or dismissing, a school superintendent. In other words, controversy comes with the job of serving on a board. To cover up this fact or to be unprepared for it makes reconciliation very difficult after a controversy has erupted.

It is important to treat controversy openly. This requires thoughtful time so that all sides can be heard. Boards also need to realize they occasionally will win and occasionally will lose. Controversy is endemic, but it need not be paralyzing. And some issues cannot be reconciled by the board—the community, through the ballot box, must be involved.

As a beginning:

☐ Find appropriate ways for individual board members to learn how to deal with conflict situations

☐ Make sure that adequate resources are available to help make decisions in controversial areas and share these with the community

☐ Make sure that all sides are heard and that board actions or its perceived opinions are not premature, in the eyes of the public

7. An effective board leads the community in matters of public education, seeking and responding to many forms of participation by the community.

In contemporary governance of public education, citizens not only participate through the election process and vote on school issues but also become involved through other forms of participation. Many boards are comfortable with citizen participation; for others it is not a question of preference but a mandate that must be fulfilled to satisfy state or federal rules.

Board members vary in their openness and ability to relate to citizen input. But despite such individual differences, effective boards will seek advice and counsel from the community and will show their sincerity by using citizen suggestions and recommendations whenever possible.

As a beginning:

☐ Establish community/parent involvement as a school district precept

☐ Develop ways to draw upon the community, from volunteer help in classrooms to business advocacy for the school district

☐ Invest in staff and resources to organize, channel and respond to community involvement with the schools

☐ Provide structure for community input into board self-assessment

8. An effective board exercises continuing oversight of education programs and their management, draws information for this purpose from many sources and knows enough to ask the right questions.

Some school boards chafe at relying exclusively on the school administration for information regarding programs and needs. Often, the board may want to supplement such information with data from other sources. Needs should be determined, resources analyzed, gaps filled—in an orderly, open manner which allows the school board to review various facets of the school program regularly and consistently.

As a beginning:

☐ Plan oversight practices and procedures with the school administration

☐ List those aspects of the education program which should be reviewed on a regular basis and develop a calendar that allows sufficient time to consider each one

☐ Keep such a listing flexible so that new programs, trends or issues are considered and added as needed

☐ Ascertain the resources for information available to the school board and determine whether they should be supplemented in any way

☐ Stay abreast of new developments in technologies that can improve information-gathering and management capabilities

9. An effective board, in consultation with its superintendent, works out and periodically reaffirms the separate areas of administrative and policy responsibilities and how these separations will be maintained.

Misunderstandings will occur unless boards work diligently to clarify who is responsible for what and where responsibilities must be shared. Legal duties usually are not the problem because these are specified. Problems arise from more subtle causes, including personality differences. Board members and superintendents, for the most part, want to do a good job. They search for effective ways to perform their duties, but there are areas which are not well understood and need clarification. This need should be recognized and given thoughtful attention.

If board members and their superintendent agree that board members can be involved heavily in administration, and all parties live up to that agreement, then such an arrangement may work effectively. Similarly, board members and their superintendent may agree that some policy proposals, developed by the staff and presented by the superintendent, will guide policy action.

Because board member turnover is high, these agreements should be reviewed periodically.

As a beginning:

☐ Analyze the area that essentially is policy and falls to the board, and the area that essentially is administrative and falls to the superintendent

☐ Anticipate the effect of any changes by discussing hypothetical situations

☐ Make sure a new consensus is developed with a new superintendent

10. An effective board, if it uses committees, determines the mission and agenda of each, ensuring coherence and coordination of policy and oversight functions.

The expertise and interests of individual board members can be used effectively on board committees. But such committees, left unguided by the full board, can become fiefdoms. The board must agree on the scope of each committee and accept leadership directives that place committee work in perspective.

Board committees should use the experience and talents of various central office (and other) staff. Further, some boards may want to go beyond school district resources and use expertise available elsewhere to supplement their work.

As a beginning:

☐ Make sure that continuing committee assignments concentrate on important policy areas, and use ad hoc committees to respond to changing needs

☐ Include committees in the board's formal operating policies

☐ Establish, with the superintendent, how staff support will be structured and assigned to committees

11. An effective board establishes policy to govern its own policymaking and policy oversight responsibilities, including explicit budget provisions to support those activities.

Making policy should not be a hit or miss activity. Careful steps should be taken, including gathering information, analyzing it, allowing for community and staff input, testing policy proposals and evaluating their implementation. Under each major step are more discrete functions, such as informing the public of a major proposal or developing a timetable and the tools to be used in evaluating the effects of a policy.

As a beginning:

☐ Develop written policies on policymaking and policy oversight

☐ Include policies and procedures to govern board committee work

☐ Allocate resources to support these activities

12. An effective board invests in its own development, using diverse approaches that address the needs of individual board members and the board as a whole.

Serving on a school board requires self-sacrifice. This voluntary workforce, receiving little if any compensation, deserves the opportunity to improve its competence. Boards should develop a policy providing for board education and development—and support it through a line item in school budgets.

Further, board development should not be reserved only for new members. It should be scheduled to involve all board members regularly and should draw upon high quality expertise and resources.

It is necessary to recognize when a board is beginning to lose cohesion and needs outside help. Numerous resources (community, school boards associations, consultants, etc.) can be enlisted to help the board through difficult times.

As a beginning:

☐ Establish board development as a policy with budgeted resources

☐ Develop high standards for board development, seeking expertise especially relevant to board needs and community expectations

☐ Educate the community to the need, value and appropriateness of devoting district resources to board development

13. An effective board establishes procedures for selecting and evaluating the superintendent. It also has procedures for evaluating itself.

A community will agree to the selection of a superintendent if it has been involved in the selection process, including the establishment of criteria and, where possible, representation in the interview stage. The process should be candid, with the board representing its community and values fairly; and the process should be conducted expertly, with the board agreeing on its priorities as well as the information it wants from candidates. Evaluation procedures should be specified.

Likewise, the regular evaluation of the board should involve the community, be conducted expertly and include a process for using the evaluation results to improve the board's functioning.

As a beginning:

☐ Develop written procedures for selection of a superintendent

☐ Develop written procedures for evaluation of the superintendent

☐ Establish policies and procedures for evaluation of the board

14. An effective board collaborates with other boards through its statewide school boards association and other appropriate groups to influence state policy and the way state leadership meets the needs of local schools.

If school boards are agents of the state—a role defined in most state constitutions—then boards should become partners in the policy-making process at the state level. Some traditional education interest groups have not been so effective as they might in the current reform efforts, probably because they have been viewed as defending the **status quo**.

Rather than react to policies and mandates, school boards could be providing wise counsel and their own agendas for education improvement and assessment that would be assured of being relevant to local needs and resources.

As a beginning:

☐ Use the collective resources of school boards to conduct surveys of needs and local exemplary education practices and to develop positions on proposed reforms

☐ Involve state legislators locally in policy discussions

☐ Anticipate trends and present recommendations before they escape local influence

☐ Seek to establish regular forums for local / state dialogues

☐ Mobilize other local stakeholders in education

15. An effective board understands the role of the media and its influence on public perceptions, develops procedures with the school administration for media contact and avoids manipulating media attention for personal gains.

Media coverage of the schools, especially of school board meetings, can be a source of tension and conflict. However, public officials, including school board members, are entrusted with *public* responsibilities and thus are subject to public scrutiny. The media—the Fourth Estate—is doing its job when it closely covers the conduct of school boards, even though boards and individual members may smart from such exposure.

Conversely, school boards can be harmed seriously by the attempt of individual board members—or the superintendent—to use the media for personal agendas, especially when such agendas are counter to the policies or sense of the board as a whole. Such individual actions can negatively affect the ability of a school board to provide leadership as seriously as can any shortcoming of the board as a whole.

As a beginning:

☐ Establish written procedures assigning the responsibilities for the chief spokesperson for the school district

☐ Establish board policies governing relationships with the media

☐ Develop an open and cooperative relationship with the media

☐ Schedule regular briefings with media executives; do not wait for a crisis to develop

Notes

1. Donald T. Alvey, Kenneth E. Underwood, and Jimmy C. Fortune, "Our Annual Look at Who You Are and What's Got You Worried," *The American School Board Journal,* January, 1986, pp. 23-27.

2. *Ibid.,* p. 23.

3. *Ibid.,* p. 23.

4. Harold L. Hodgkinson, *All One System: The Demographics of Education Kindergarten through Graduate School,* Institute for Educational Leadership, 1985.

5. Louis Harris, *A Survey of the Reaction of the American and Top Business Executives to the Report on Public Education by the Task Force on Teaching as a Profession of the Carnegie Forum on Education and the Economy,* Carnegie Forum on Education and the Economy, August, 1986, 47p.

6. Luvern L. Cunningham and Joseph Hentges, (Eds.), *American School Superintendents, 1982, A Full Report,* AASA, Rosslyn, VA, 1982.

7. National School Boards Association and American Association of School Administrators, *Survey of School Boards/Superintendent Relations,* Alexandria/Arlington, VA, 1986.

8. Luvern L. Cunningham and Joseph Hentges, (Eds.), *American School Superintendents, 1982, A Full Report,* AASA, Rosslyn, VA, 1982.

9. Luvern L. Cunningham, *The Ohio State University Survey of State School Boards Associations,* (a study in process).

10. William Harvey Ditze, *An Analysis of Board of Education Professional Development Experiences Related to Selected Elements of Board Functions,* University of Michigan, Ann Arbor, MI, 1979.

11. Cynthia Anne Bizozowski, *Perceived School Board Training Needs,* University of Michigan, Ann Arbor, MI, 1981.

Bibliography

Cynthia Anne Bizozowski, *Perceived School Board Training Needs*, University of Michigan, Ann Arbor, MI, 1981.

William L. Boyd, *Community Status and Conflict in Suburban School Politics*, Beverly Hills, CA, Sage, 1975.

William L. Boyd, "School Board–Administrative Staff Relationships," in *Understanding School Boards*, Peter Cistone (ed.), Lexington, MA, Lexington Books, 1975.

Raymond Callahan, "The American Board of Education, 1789-1960," in *Understanding School Boards*, Peter Cistone (ed.), Lexington, MA, Lexington Books, 1975.

Roald F. Campbell, Luvern L. Cunningham, Raphael O. Nystrand, and Michael D. Usdan, *The Organization and Control of American Schools*, Fifth Edition, Charles E. Merrill Publishing Company, 1985, Columbus, OH, Chap. 8, pp. 167-194.

Lila N. Carol, *A Study of Methods for Evaluating Chief School Officers in Local School Districts*, New Jersey School Boards Association, Trenton, NJ, 1972.

Peter J. Cistone, ed., *Understanding School Boards*, Lexington, MA, Lexington Books, 1975.

Peter J. Cistone, "The Socialization of School Board Members," *Educational Administration Quarterly*, 13, no. 2, 1977.

Peter J. Cistone, "School Boards," in *Encyclopedia of Educational Research, Fifth Edition*, Harold Mitzel (ed.), New York, The Free Press, 1982, Vol. 4, pp. 1637-1645.

George S. Counts, *The Social Composition of Boards of Education: A Study in the Social Control of Public Education*, Chicago, IL, The University of Chicago, 1927.

Luvern L. Cunningham, "The School Board," in *Excellence in Education*, John Mangieri (ed.), Texas Christian University Press, 1985.

Luvern L. Cunningham and Joseph Hentges, (eds.), *American School Superintendents, 1982, A Full Report*, American Association of School Administrators, Rosslyn, VA, 1982.

Luvern L. Cunningham, *The Ohio State University Survey of State School Board Associations*, (a study in process).

William Dickinson (ed.), *New Dimensions in School Board Leadership: A Seminar Report and Workbook*, Evanston, IL, National School Boards Association, Inc., 1969.

William Harvey Ditzel, *An Analysis of Board of Education Professional Development Experiences Related to Selected Elements of Board Functions*, University of Michigan, Ann Arbor, MI, 1979.

Craig Gifford, *Boardmanship: A Handbook for School Board Members*, Westerville, OH, The Ohio Department of Education and The Ohio School Boards Association, 1976.

Keith Goldhammer, *The School Board*, New York, The Center for Applied Research in Education, Inc., 1964.

William J. Grimshaw, *Union Rule in the Schools*, Lexington, MA, Lexington Books, 1979.

Neal Gross, *Who Runs Our Schools?* New York, John Wiley & Sons, Inc., 1958.

James W. Guthrie, *Public Control of Public Schools*, Public Affairs Report, University of California, Institute of Governmental Studies, 1974.

Joseph Hentges, *The Politics of Superintendent-School Board Linkages: A Study of Power, Participation, and Control*, Ph.D. Dissertation, The Ohio State University, 1984.

M. Kent Jennings, "Parental Grievances and School Politics," *Public Opinion Quarterly*, 32, 1968.

Norman D. Kerr, "The School Board as an Agency of Legitimation," *Sociology of Education*, 38, 1964.

George Albert Leonard, *Descriptive Studies of a Superintendent: Perceptions of Inservice Training Programs for School Board Members in the United States and Canada*, Wayne State University, Detroit, MI, 1978.

Dale Mann, *The Politics of Administrative Representation*, Lexington, MA, Lexington Books, 1976.

David W. Minar, "The Community Basis of Conflict in School System Politics," *American Sociological Review*, 31, 1966.

David W. Minar, *Educational Decision-Making in Suburban Communities*, (Cooperative Research Project No. 2440). Evanston, IL, Northwestern University, 1966.

Paul E. Peterson, *School Politics Chicago Style*, Chicago, University of Chicago Press, 1976.

Charles Reeves, *School Boards: Their Status, Functions and Activities*, New York: Prentice Hall, Inc., 1954.

Jesse Sears, "School Board Control–The Necessary Tools and Procedures," in *Educational Administration & Supervision, Including Teacher Training*, William Bagley, Thomas Briggs, Boyd Bode, Gordon Hullfish, and H.E. Buchholz (eds.), Baltimore: Warwick & York, Inc., 1942, Vol. 28, pp. 561-580.

John Neil Shuster, *An Assessment of Perceived Needs and Participation of Southwestern Michigan Public School Board Members in Local, Regional and Statewide Programs of Inservice Education*, Michigan State University, East Lansing, MI, 1980.

Michael P. Smith, "Elite Theory and Policy Analysis, The Politics of Education in Suburbia," *Journal of Politics,* 36, 1974.

Leigh Stelzer, "Institutionalizing Conflict Response: The Case of School Boards," *Social Science Quarterly* 55, no. 2 1974.

Edward Tuttle, *School Board Leadership in America*, Danville, IL, The Interstate Printers and Publishers, 1963.

Michael D. Usdan, "The Future Viability of the School Board," in *Understanding School Boards*, Peter J. Cistone (ed.), Lexington, MA, Lexington Books, 1975.

Tyll van Geel, *Authority to Control the School Program*, Lexington, MA, Lexington Books, 1976.

Frederick Wirt and Michael Kirst, *The Politics of Education: Schools in Conflict*, Berkeley, McCutchan Publishing Corporation, 1982.

Harmon Zeigler, "School Board Research: The Problems and the Prospects," in *Understanding School Boards*, Peter J. Cistone (ed.), Lexington, MA, Lexington Books, 1975.

Harmon Zeigler and Kent Jennings, *Governing American Schools*, North Scituate, MA, Duxbury, 1974.

"...this report throws sudden
and welcome light
on that dark island of
American governance,
the institution
that everyone knows of
but few understand:
the school board."

Neal Peirce,
Contributing Editor
"The National Journal"

"This report should be read
by everyone concerned
about how things
actually get done in
school districts."

Nellie C. Weil,
President
Thomas A. Shannon,
Executive Director
National School Boards Association